150

D1480495

WORKING WITH POLICE AGENCIES

The Inter-relations Between
Law Enforcers and the Behavioral
Scientist

COMMUNITY-CLINICAL
PSYCHOLOGY SERIES

WORKING WITH POLICE AGENCIES

Volume III of a Continuing Series in
Community-Clinical Psychology

Edited by

Robert Cohen, Director
Institute of Community Development
Syracuse, New York

Robert P. Sprafkin, Coordinator
Veterans Administration
Day Treatment Center
Syracuse, New York

Sidney Oglesby, Associate Director
Institute for Community Development
Syracuse, New York

William L. Claiborn, Director
Prince William
Community Mental Health Center
Manassas, Virginia

HUMAN SCIENCES PRESS
SUBSIDIARY OF BEHAVIORAL PUBLICATIONS INC.
72 FIFTH AVENUE, NEW YORK, N.Y. 10011

Library of Congress Catalog Number 75-17450

ISBN: 0-87705-224-7

Printed in the United States of America

6789 987654321

Library of Congress Cataloging in Publication
Data

Cohen, Robert
     Police & Behavioral Sciences
New York   Human Sciences Press
1976 August

(Community Clinical Psychology Series, Vol. III)

                    30 may 75

For those police officers we have met who
continually put into practice the principles
of community psychology and especially for
Manny Leone and Warren Darby.

CONTRIBUTING AUTHORS

Dennis Angelini
Career Counseling Project
Educational Development
Corporation
Providence, Rhode Island
02903

John D. Burchard
Psychology Department
University of Vermont
Burlington, Vermont 05401

William Claiborn
Prince William Community
Mental Health Center
Manassas, Virginia

Robert Cohen
Institute for Community
Development
204 East Jefferson Street
Syracuse, New York 13202

Charles W. Dean
Sociology Department
University of Harford
Hartford, Connecticut 06117

Paul T. Harig
Psychology Department
University of Vermont
Burlington, Vermont 05401

Joseph T. Himmelsbach
Hutchings Psychiatric
Center
Syracuse, New York 13210

Leonard M. Lansky
Community Psychology
Institute
University of Cincinnati
Cincinnati, Ohio 45221

John F. O'Connor
New York State Department
of Motor Vehicles
Syracuse, New York 13202

Sidney Oglesby
Institute for Community
Development
204 East Jefferson Street
Syracuse, New York 13202

W. Brendan Reddy
Community Psychology
Institute
University of Cincinnati
Cincinnati, Ohio 45221

Addison W. Sommerville
Psychology Department
California State University
Sacramento, California 95819

Robert P. Sprafkin
Veterans Administration Hospital
Syracuse, New York 13210

Robert E. Tournier
Department of Sociology
The College of Charleston
Charleston, South Carolina
29401

Phillip York
Youth Services Division
Sacramento Police Department
Sacramento, California
85814

CONTENTS

SECTION V:

SUMMARY AND CONCLUSIONS

PREFACE

The continuing series in Community-
Clinical Psychology has been developed in
response to the often expressed need to
prepare social scientists for work in community
settings. Based on the Annual Symposium on
Current Issues in Community Psychology, this
series has previously addressed itself to the
issues of school intervention and crisis
intervention. The present has evolved from
a symposium entitled, "Working with Police
Agencies," which brought together both social
science practitioners and police officials in
order to more fully explore the applications of
social science in improving the human relations
aspects of police services/ The Symposium
was designed to enable participants to:

1) gain a better understanding of the
problems involved in police work;

2) learn new approaches to improving
relations with police agencies, and between
police and citizens;

3) improve police and citizens' abilities
to evaluate police services.

This symposium, sponsored by the Institute
for Community Development (an independent non
profit organization), the Central New York

Regional Academy for Police Training and the
Clinical Psychology Training Program of
Syracuse University, was attended by more
than 50 individuals, representing social
science and police agencies throughout the
United States. During the three day Symposium,
the participants listened and discussed
presentations, attended workshops, participated
in simulation exercises and conversed with
each other informally.

The pages which follow include the
edited version of papers presented at the
Symposium, as well as several original
contributions written especially for this
volume. In all cases, the primary guiding
principle for selection of papers has been
whether the material would contribute to the
reader's understanding of the practical problems,
issues and methodologies involved in developing
a working relationship between police and
social scientists: Effective approaches for
providing consultation to police agencies;
program development in the areas of crisis
intervention and community relations; and
methods of assessing and evaluating police
services.

A number of people have contributed to
the development of this book. We particularly
want to acknowledge the assistance of Howard
Day, Director of the Central New York Regional
Academy for Police Training, Lee Smith,
Assistant Dean for Community and Mid=Career
Programs, University College, Syracuse University,
Warren Darby of the Syracuse Police Department
and Karen Harrington, Kathy Young and Roland
Yorke of the Institute for Community Development.

R.C.
R.P.S.
S.O.
W.L.C.
November, 1974

INTRODUCTION

In recent years the work of police officers and police departments across the country has come to the forefront as a public issue. This public and widespread attention to, and evaluation of, police work has emanated from various levels of society and has been directed toward numerous aspects concerning the functions of police. Often the attention has begun a criticism; criticisms of the types and quality of services offered by police departments; criticisms about the responsiveness of police to the perceived needs of various segments of the community; criticisms of the organization of police departments, the use of force by police, the adequacy of training for police officers, to name just a few areas (Clark, 1971; Garmire, 1972).

Two major themes that seem to have emerged from the onslaught of examinations of police work are those of *responsiveness* and *accountability*. Responsiveness to community needs appears to have paralleled, historically, other examinations of previously unchallenged public practices. Certainly the impact of school desegregation, the Civil Rights movement, and the poverty programs of the '50s and '60s helped sensitize segments of society to the possibility of examining and perhaps changing some of the institutions

1

of society, including the police (Banton, 1964). And along with the awareness that institutions might be changed to be more responsive to all segments of the community, was an awareness that the language used in describing the functions of agencies or institutions might take on difference meanings for different segments of the community. For example, all segments of the community might agree that a major function of the police should be "peace keeping." However, many citizens, sensitized to differences in meanings and consequences of meanings, became aware that "peace keeping" might have different behavioral implications for different strata or groups within society (Ahern, 1972).

The demand for accountability most likely arose along with a greater public awareness of the discrepancy between the (strict, quasimilitary) internal accountability within virtually all police departments and the (often loose or nonexistent) external accountability to community groups, courts, or other legal avenues. Again, as with other institutions in society, there was a demand for more public examination, and questioning of tradition-bound practices which ultimately would effect public service.

Social scientists have long addressed themselves to issues involving the assessment and evaluation of individuals or organizations, as well as to issues involving relationships amoung community groups, and related to social concerns. Thus, when demands in terms of evaluation and of responsiveness to community needs began to be felt by police, it seemed natural that social scientists would be called upon, or would volunteer their services, to help police meet these demands.

We have, then, an emerging dialogue

between police and social scientists. As with other types of dialogue, we become concerned with several important questions: Do the parties in the dialogue understand each other? Can they? Are they speaking the same language directed toward the same objects of study? Are the parties antagonistic? Can they work together appropriately and productively? Are they the proper parties to the dialogue? What unique contributions can each make that some other discipline could not? Does it promise to be a continuing dialogue rather than a marriage of convenience and necessity? What should be the appropriate working relationships among the dialogue members?

These are, in essence, the kinds of questions that prompted the present volume. The following chapters will explore such concerns as consultation styles and approaches, program development, and assessment and evaluation techniques. It is hoped that these presentations will help to answer some of the basic questions we have about the feasibility, desirability, directions, and likely outcomes of the collaborations between police and social scientists.

REFERENCES

1. Ahern, J. F. *Police in Trouble.*New York: Hawthorne, 1972.

2. Banton, M. *The Policeman in the Community.* New York: Basic Books, 1964

3. Clark, R. *Crime in America, Observations on its Nature, Causes, Prevention and Control.* New York: Simon and Schuster, 1970.

4. Garmire, B. et al. *The Police and the Community.* Committee for Economic Development, Supplementary Paper. Baltimore: John Hopkins University Press, 1972.

SECTION I:

INTRODUCTION

1. A CHALLENGE TO CHANGE

John F. O'Connor

Since the editors of this book are all social scientists, it seemed appropriate to include in the introductory section the perspective of someone who has spent most of his professional career working as a police officer. John F. O'Connor worked for 22 years as a law enforcement officer in New York City before coming to Syracuse, New York, where he has served as Chief of Police, Executive Director of the New York State Joint Legislature Committee on Crime, its Causes, Control and Effect on Society, and currently is Deputy Commissioner of the New York State Department of Motor Vehicles.

In his paper, O'Connor describes some of the problems police are regularly confronted with in the performance of their duties, and stresses the need for social scientists to aid police officers in learning to cope with the complex community affairs they encounter. However, he goes beyond this frequently discussed area, and urges social scientists and police officials to view the police agency as a component of the criminal justice system, which cannot be considered in isolation from the rest of that system. The legislative units, the courts and the corrections system all have an impact upon the manner in which police agencies

*function, and the ways in which these agencies
are responded to by the public.   O'Connor
argues that without significant changes in
all aspects of the criminal justice system,
any attempts to improve the performance of
police agencies will be superficial and
relatively ineffectual.*

The police, almost half a million of
them serving about "forty thousand agencies
that spend more than two and a half billion
dollars a year" (Katzenbach, 1967, p. 91),
are the part of the criminal justice system
that is in direct daily contact with crime
and criminals and with the public. Perhaps
the most unique aspect of police work is that
it's generally performed in the open arena of
public observation, on the street where
instantaneous decisions must be made and action
taken without benefit of useful advice or time
for research. "Police work" is much more than
a phrase that produces an image in the minds of
some observer of the occasional public "contest
between a policeman and a criminal in which
the party with the stronger arm or the craftier
wit prevails" (Katzenbach, 1967, p. 91).
Police work is distinctively important, complex,
noticeable, and delicate because of "increasing
crime, increasing social unrest, and increasing
public sensitivity to both" (Katzenbach, 1967,
p. 91).

A great majority of the situations in which
the police intervene cannot be interpreted,
and are not so interpreted by the police themselves, as criminal situations calling for
arrest, prosecution, trial and punishment.
In many of these cases the police intervene
because the public requests intervention, or
because the incident is clearly a public
nuisance requiring intervention to prevent
the development of a crime. "Many situations

involve people who need help whether they want
it or not" (Katzenbach, 1967, p.91). Many of
them involve conduct that, while unlawful,
cannot be prevented or deterred to any great
degree by the traditional means now available.
Many situations, whether or not they involve
unlawful conduct, may pose the threat of
serious public disorder. Much of police work
is seeing to it that the undesirable extreme,
public disorder or serious crime, does not
come about. This means that the police are
thrust in a most intimate, personal way into
the lives and problems of citizens of all
kinds.

It is impossible to exaggerate the
closeness or the variety of the contacts
between the police and the community. Policemen deal with people who are at one time
aggressive yet vulnerable; when they are
angry, desperate, drunk, violent, or when they
are ashamed. Every police action can affect
in some way someone's dignity, or self-respect,
or sense of privacy, or constitutional rights.

A common situation that illustrates the
complexity, delicacy, and frustration, of
much police work is the matrimonial dispute.
The capacity of the police to deal effectively
with such a highly personal matter as conjugal
disharmony is extremely limited. Arrest is
unlikely to result in a prosecution or a
reconciliation. Removing one of the parties
from the scene is at best a temporary truce,
likely to be broken and leading to a return
visit by the police. Referring to court in
the morning is a bluff that is frequently
called (and ignored) on the spot. Handling
marital disputes is a skill possessed by few
people, in or out of police work. Family
fights are one of the leading causes of
homicides. Family intervention as convention-
ally practiced is one of the leading causes

of assaults on policemen.

Since police action is so often so personal,it is inevitable that the public is of two minds about the police: Most men both welcome official protection and resent official interference. The way the police perform their duties depends to a large extent upon which state of mind predominates; whether the police are thought of as protectors or oppressors, as friends or enemies. Yet policemen, who as a rule have been well trained to perform such procedures as searching a person for weapons, transporting a suspect to the stationhouse, taking fingerprints, writing arrest reports, and testifying in court, have received little guidance from legislatures, city administrations, or their own superiors,in handling thse intricate, intimate human situations. The organization of police departments and the training of policemen are forcused almost entirely on the apprehension and prosecution of criminals. What a policeman does, or should do, instead of making an arrest or in order to avoid making an arrest, or in a situation in which he may not make an arrest, is rarely discussed. The peace keeping and service activities, which consume the majority of police time, receive too little consideration.

"Finally more than public attitudes toward the police and, by extension toward the law, are influenced by the way any given policeman performs his duties. Every Supreme Court decision that has redefined or limited such important and universal police procedures as search and seizure, interrogation of suspects, arrest, and the use of informants has been a decision about the way a specific policeman or group of policemen handled a specific situation. Most of the recent big city riots were touched off by commonplace street

encounters between policemen and citizens.
In short, the way any policeman exercises
the personal discretion that is an inescapable
part of his job can, and occasionally does,
have an immediate bearing on the peace and
safety of an entire community, or a long-range
bearing on the work of all policemen every
where" (Katzenbach, 1967, p.92).

Only on rare occasions have practitioners
in the social science disciplines brought
their skill and knowledge to the conference
table and shared it with police officers. For
far too long, the police have been systematically
excluded from acquiring basic skills in social
science. The exclusion has been brought about
by myopic police leaders and by a small but
powerful group of social science leaders who
viewed the police as a brutal anachronism
which should be abolished.

Fortunately, symposiums such as the
current one are becoming more frequent and
police are acquiring skills necessary for
coping with the rapid social change occurring
in our urban communities.

I would urge both police and social
science practitioners, that while in the process
of deliberating about police problems, improved
police public relations and improved evaluation
of police services it is essential to bear in
mind the problems of all the agencies in the
criminal justice system.

The police can stand improvement, what
institution created by mortal man cannot,
but it is a fact that the police have led the
way among all the units of the system at
seeking self improvement. It must be
remembered that no lasting solution of the
problems of the police can be achieved in a
vacuum, that is to say, without relating

problem and solution to the interaction of the
police with the courts and correction system.

The police can improve their capacity to
handle nonarrest cases. But there is convincing
evidence that it is worse than useless to
improve the present capacity of the police to
effect arrests in criminal cases. Improving the
'quality of arrests is necessary. Improving the
number of arrests, without fundamental changes
in our courts and corrections system, will be
self defeating.

In 1970, the police in New York State
effected 114,302 felony arrests. The
prosecutorial services produced 30,137 felony
indictments from these arrests, and arrest to
indictment ratio of 28.1 per cent, less than
one third. The average arrest to indictment
ratio for the ten year period from 1960 through
1969 was 32 per cent with a high of 41 per cent
in 1960 and a low of 28 per cent in 1967.

From the 30,137 indictments, prosecutorial
services achieved 10,835 felony convictions,
a conviction to indictment ratio of 36 per cent.
The average felony conviction to indictment
ratio from 1960 through 1969 was 32 per cent
with a high of 37 per cent in '60 and'63 and
a low 27 per cent in '66. The conviction to
arrest ratio is 10.5 per cent while the 1960-69
average ratio was 10 per cent with a high of
15 per cent in '60 and a low of 8 per cent in
'67. Viewed on a line graph over the ten year
period, convictions and indictments describe
a practically straight line while the arrest
line soars off the top of the chart. In 1970,
there were about 1,000 of the 30,000 indictments
tried to a conclusion. Over 90 per cent of
convictions are achieved via the guilty plea
bargain process. The significance of these
figures to police performance is in the
virtually constant relationship of arrests to

indictments to convictions. It is very
questionable whether even improved quality
in police arrest would alter the structure.
The rest of the system is simply suffering
from over capacity and under performance.

The criminal court is the central,
crucial institution in the criminal justice
system. It is the institution around which
the rest of the system has developed and to
which the rest of the system is in large
measure responsible. It regulates the flow
of criminal process under goverance of the
law. The activities of the police are
limited or shaped by the rules and procedures
of the court. The work of the correctional
system is determined by the court's sentence.

"In 1967 the president's commission on
law enforcement and the administration of
justice found that 'very little observation
of the administration of criminal justice in
operation is required to reach the conclusion
that it suffers from basic ills'"(Katzenbach,
1967, p. 128). The Commission found further
that "the traditional methods of court
administration have not been equal to managing
huge caseloands. Law enforcement effectiveness
is lost as courts are unable to deal properly
with the defendants brought into them"
(Katzenbach, 1967, p. 127).

Five years later, and after the expenditure
of huge sums, almost one billion dollars for a
whole plethora of projects ranging from blue
blazer jackets for policemen to computerized
unit locator systems, very little has changed.
Indeed, there is good reason for believing the
situation to have gotten worse. One reason for
his is the tendency of some authoritative
judicial leaders to attribute the obvious
mistakes of the court system to the "fundamental,
complicated, interrelated and unresolved

social problems of the times." Surely this
is an exercise in tortured logic. The existence
of social problems is, in large measure, the
reason for the existence of the courts.
Society charges the courts with an educational
and controlling role in articulating the
view of the community on the complex
relationship of the individual to the larger
society of which he forms a part.

Tracking judicial vagaries on the need
for court reform is a fascinating adventure
which at times could become amusing, if the
stakes were not so high. Recently an appellate
justice was quoted in a local newspaper as
stating "that blaming the ills of the court
on judicial working hours or lawyers' propensity
for oratory is like a physician worrying about
a skin blemish with a patient in cardiac arrest."
Quite parenthetically, one may note that skin
blemishes sometimes grow to terminal cancer
proportions and most patients reach a point of
cardiac arrest as a result of clogged and
inefficient arteries. In the same report the
justice was quoted to say that "justice is far
too important to be left exclusively to the
technician of the law. Should the citizenry
come to the conclusion that we legalists have
built up a process that is inadequate or
archaic or if they think the system does not
meet the test of utility and fairness, we must
remember that they have the ultimate right
and power to change it.

But if it is a fair assumption to observe
that the learned justice, at least by implication,
suggested that the court system is in some
stage of cardiac arrest and further to assume
that he is aware of the five-year-old finding
of the President's Commission that the "courts
are unable to deal properly with the defendants
brought into them" (Katzenbach, 1967, p.127),
then one is compelled to wonder what it will

take to convince the justice that the citizenry *has* come to the conclusion that our court system is inadequate and archaic and does *not* meet the test of social utility and fairness.

To illustrate, the New York State Joint Legislative Committee on Crime, Its Causes, Control & Effect on Society found that, as previously noted, 90% of criminal convictions are obtained by the process of guilty plea bargaining. At least 75% of the inmates of our correctional system plead guilty to a lesser charge than the one for which they were arrested - some plead to a crime they had, in fact, now committed; some plead to a non-existent crime. The climactic act in the guilty plea bargain process comes when the accused stands before the judge, in the presence of the Assistant District Attorney and his counsel and indicates for the record that he is entering his plea freely, willingly and voluntarily and that he is *not* doing so because of any promises or considerations made to him. The tragic wrong of this charade is that all three actors in the drama, and the deprivation of liberty should always be a dramatic moment, know that a promise or consideration is *precisely* the reason for the plea of guilty. It is little wonder that the credibility of the criminal justice system is practically non-existent among those who have been processed by it.

Almost all of the information on guilty plea bargaining in our courts is derived from the practitioners in the criminal justice system and the incomplete case records which indicate the disposition of cases. Obviously, the operators of a system are seldom able to produce a totally objective evaluation of the effectiveness of the system they manage and in fact, they are most reluctant to divulge information likely to reflect unfavorably on

their performance. The records maintained
are so lacking in detail and completeness as
to preclude anything but a dark and convoluted
picture of the relationship between plea
bargaining and justice.

The Committee decided to explore hitherto
uncharted areas, to examine the end product
of the efforts of the justice system, the
prisoner. He is, after all, in a unique
position to relate the overall impace of the
system. Before Attica erupted, Committee
staff went to Attica, and to Auburn, Greenhaven
and Ossining Correctional Institutions and
distributed 600 questionnaires on a random
sample basis to the inmates. Over 100 in-depth
interviews were conducted and tape-recorded.
The results obtained were as follows:

1)   88% indicated that they had been
persistently solicited to enter a guilty plea.

2)   87% insisted that the sentencing
judge was not only aware of the deal but
frequently participated in the negotiations.

3)   91% said that they wrongly denied
that a promise had been made to induce the
plea, because of prompting and direction from
their attorney.

4)   45% insisted that the State of New
York *broke* the Guilty Plea Bargain.

5)   72% expressed total dissatisfaction
with their lawyer and his efforts on their
behalf.

6)   58% indicated that, based on their
experience they would now go to trial instead
of plea.

There are two salient results of this

study. The first is that the prison population consists larely of dangerous offenders - 66% of the sample had committed crimes against the person. The implication of that figure in terms of preventing and controlling prison unrest or disorder needs no enlargement. The second point is that there are probably at least 4,000 inmates who are convinced that they have been victimized by an institution of society. No program of rehabilitation, no matter how carefully conceived, is likely to redirect a prisoner with such a conviction.

Finally, what about our correctional system? It is reasonable to conclude that society can seek to protect itself from internal attack by deterring offenders through punishment for such attacks. If society has that right, then it also has a duty to seek the rehabilitation of offenders and - largely from self-interest - return them to useful, productive lives in our communities.

The record of successful rehabilitation leaves much to be desired. A study of inmates released between 1911 and 1922 showed that 32% of the men who could be traced over a 15 year period *repeatedly* committed serious crimes during this period and many others did so on an intermittent basis. A study of California parolees released between 1946 and 1949 found that 43% had been reimprisoned by the end of 1952. A study of New York State prison inmates receiving mandatory releases between July, 1962 and June, 1964, disclosed that 56% were rearrested within five years. A study of United State Correction System mandatory releases in 1963 disclosed that 74% had been rearrested by the end of 1968.

A picture becomes bleaker when we consider that the actual amount of crime in the United States is several times the amount actually

reported and that the police apprehend
criminal offenders at a discouragingly low
overall ratio to offenses reported.   Add to
that the fact that the average daily population,
adult and juvenile, in corrections in 1965
was 1,282,386.   Projections for 1975 estimate
that the average daily population of corrections
will be 1,841,000, an increase of 43 per cent
(Katzenbach, 1967, p.160).   We have had ample
warning that the correction system is not
correcting, at least not very well, for a
whole variety of reasons.

Significant improvements can be made in
our criminal justice system, changes which could
do much to reduce crime, eliminate injustices
and win the respect and cooperation of all
citizens.   But the improvements can only come
about if the practitioners in the system develop
a "willingness to change".   More than that,
they must be challenged to change and given
the resources to effect change.

The emerging presence of dialogue between
social scientists and police shows that one
unit of the system is willing to change.   But
producing a fragmented, comparmentalized program
of change is doomed to failure.   By definition,
a system is an orderly arrangement of parts
into a whole, a combination based on a rational
principle.

We do well to meet, to discuss, to comment,
and to exchange opinions on the police.   But
we should not stop there.   We should carry
our interest into the whole system - so that
the phrase "equal justice under law" can
achieve the fullness of meaning envisioned
by our founding fathers.

REFERENCES

Katzenbach, N. (Chairman). The challenge
     of crime in a free society, A Report
     by the President's Commission on Law
     Enforcement and Administration of
     Justice, February, 1967.

SECTION II:

THE SOCIAL SCIENTIST AS CONSULTANT

TO POLICE AGENCIES

2. ISSUES AND ROLES

Robert P. Sprafkin and Robert Cohen

*Once a social scientist has expressed
an interest in serving as a consultant, and a
police agency has decided it has a need for
assistance, the next step is to determine the
specific type of consultation and service that
should be provided. One of the primary purposes
of this book is to enable the reader to become
aware of the range of consulting services that
are feasible. Most of the articles provide
examples, suggestions and questions related
to a specific theme or role. This paper, by
Robert Sprafkin and Robert Cohen, is intended
as prelude to the more comprehensive presentations that follow. The authors attempt to
provide an overview of the types of roles that
consultants may undertake and some of the
issues associated with each role. While they
do not advocate any particular role, Sprafkin
and Cohen stress that the consultant and
police agency should carefully scrutinize the
needs of the agency and skills of the consultant
before formally initiating a working relationship.
Six guidelines are presented to assist in the
development and assessment of a consultation
relationship.*

In recent years the number of consultative
relationships between social scientists,

19

particularly those with backgrounds in the mental health professions, and police departments has increased greatly. While this is no doubt largely due to the increased funding that has become available for the programmatic changes entailing the use of social scientist consultants, it has also been responsive to some other trends among the ranks of both the police and social scientists. First, there has been a mandate for change in police practices, both on a national and a local community level. Change has often been talked about in terms of better selection and training of police officers, better delivery of services or more civilian voice in police practices. Second, with these mandates for changes in practices came the realization among police administrators that these innovations could not be generated from within, relying solely on existing talent. Rather, they felt the need to turn to civilian consultants whose expertise was already established in these areas.

The complementary trend within the ranks of social scientists has been most broadly articulated as the Community Psychology movement. This has been marked by an effort to move out of the laboratory and classroom and to deal directly with socially relevant issues; to abandon the doctor-patient relationship in favor of working with organizations or systems in hopes of having a wider impact; of moving away from the task of treating problems that have already occurred toward the goal of identifying and preventing problems *before* they occur; of working with the institutions of society in an effort to help them become more supportive of growth and change rather than contributing to the probable causes of social and psychological problems. Thus, social scientists, particularly those caught up in the Community Psychology movement, were ripe for entering into consultative relationships with police.

While the specific types of consultative
relationships between social scientists and
police vary, certain dimensions and guidelines
about the consultant's role and style have been
articulated. Lippitt (1962) presents guidelines
concerning social scientists' consultative
behaviors with organizations. The awareness
of and adherence to these guidelines can serve
as a standard against which specific types of
social scientist-police consultation may be
evaluated. The guidelines include:

1) The consultation relationship should
be defined as a voluntary one between a
professional helper (consultant) and a system
which needs help. Such a relationship should
be perceived as temporary by both parties.
The consultant should not be a part of the
organization being helped, but should remain
an outsider.

2) The first task for the consultant is
to identify the problem, its source, and what
maintains it.

3) The consultant must identify his own
motivations for becoming involved in the
particular consultative relationship.

4) The consultant must assess the client-
organization's motivation to change (or to
resist change).

5) The consultant must assess his own
abilities and resources for giving the help
that is needed.

6) The consultant must establish a
consulting relationship with the organization
which should include helping the client-
organization develop and awareness of its

needs, establishing a trial period when
possible, and establishing a relationship
with the total organization rather than with
one person or group (Lippitt, 1962).

In light of these guidelines it is well
to examine the types of consultative relationships
social scientists have assumed with police
departments in recent years. Clearly, many of
these roles have not evolved as a result of
extensive planning, but rather in response to
immediate, pressing needs. The questions that
must be asked, both by social scientists and
police, have to do with the adequacy of these
relationships. Are consultants being used most
effectively, and, if not, how can the relationship be improved?

Some of the consultative roles and functions
that social scientists have served with the
police are:

1) *Counseling and Psychotherapy*. This
function is perhaps most congruent with the
widespread image of what social scientists,
specifically those coming from mental health
fields, have to offer, It is also true that
seeking counseling or psycho-therapy for personal
or marital problems may be viewed as a sign of
personal weakness and inadequacy (and a source
of embarassment) by a large segment of the
population, including many police officers.
And, in terms of the spirit of the Community
Psychology movement, this role has the least
potential for *prevention,*but rather is one
of traditional *treatment* (tertiary prevention
in Caplan's (1962) terminology). Nevertheless,
it is a role that the social scientist -
consultant has assumed, and will no doubt
continue to assume in the future. With this
role it is particularly important that the
consultant's autonomy, both in terms of physical
location and professional confidentiality,

be established. That is, he cannot serve
both the needs of his clients (individual
police officers) and the needs of the organization at the same time, when, indeed, the two
may be in conflict. While he may be funded
by the department his primary responsibility
must be to each client. Likewise, it is
advisable that he not have his office in the
same building as the organization for similar
reasons of confidentiality.

   2) *Screening, Testing, Selection*.
Consultants, particularly psychologists and
psychiatrists, have been widely employed in
screening new applicants and in advising on a
variety of personnel decisions (promotion,
demotion, deselection) within police departments.
This may involve the use of psychological tests,
(aptitude, interest, personality, and/or
intelligence) and diagnostic interviews. Often
it involves the consultant as the objective,
expert resource for making or justifying
otherwise difficult personnel actions. While
this often casts a cloak of legitimacy over
the personnel decision making process, the
adequacy of psychological test utilization has
not been universally accepted for employment
with the police. One major reasons for this is
the lack of precise definitions as to what is
being predicted. While tests and diagnostic
interviews may be successful in identifying
overtly psychotic individuals, their ability
to identify persons who might prove to be
excessively brutal, racist, or who otherwise
operate poorly under pressure has not been
established. Also, the consultant who involves
himself in making personnel decisions may not
be able to operate in other advisory roles
with the organization because of presumed
conflicts of interest.

   3) *Research, Program Development, Program
Evaluation*. Many social scientists come to

police agencies with considerable backgrounds
and expertise in research design and implementation and organizational development.   The role
of research consultant, program designer, or
program evaluator is also consistent with the
previously discussed values of institutional
changes of focusing on prevention rather than
treatment.   These are talents that are typically
not represented within the police department.
And, the consultant can usually be employed on
a project-specific basis (e. g.,designing a
particular program, evaluating a particular
service).   Yet the consultant's views and
those of the agency may not be congruent
(Pepinsky, 1976) and may lead to differing
definitions of the task.   Or, when the evaluation does not reflect favorably on the particular
department there may be implicit pressure to
devalue, compromise, or ignore the objectivity
of the research (Oglesby, et. al.1974).   This
is not to say that researchers have always been
forthright in their dealings with police
agencies.   In many instances, mutual lack of
trust seems to exist, based on real or stereo-
typed experiences with the other party.

4) *Education and Training* Many social
scientists consultants have academic experience
in teaching, training, and supervision.
Virtually all police departments have educational
and training needs.   Often the police training
program has included in it courses or lectures
in such social science areas as psychology,
sociology, criminology, etc. Frequently the
social scientist is brought in as the expert in
one of these fields. Anecdotal evidence is so
overwhelming that the social scientist/instructor
and his students often encounter conflict, or
at least an apathetic standoff.   To the police
trainees the social scientist is often viewed
as an abstract, ivory tower academician, who
may know theory but does not know the realities
of the street.   To the social scientist/

instructor the recruits are most often viewed
as rather dull, apathetic or hostile students
who are only in class because they are forced
to be there. Perhaps social scientists need
to consider whether traditional teaching methods
are appropriate in the situation.

Other types of training involvement are
becoming increasingly common for social scientists.
Instead of functioning as direct line instructors
in police training classes, many social scientists
have begun to consult in such roles as supervisor
of other trainers and instructors, who are frequently
drawn from the ranks of the police force. In
addition, social scientists, particularly those
with mental health backgrounds, have begun to serve
as supervisors of programs dealing with family
crisis intervention, delinquency, drug abuse and
related social problems. (Bard, 1970; Phelps,
Schwartz, and Littman, 1971). Here their role is
that of trainer/supervisor of those police officers
who are, and will continue to be in the field.

Another type of training involvment which
has emerged for social scientists in recent
years is that of human relations trainer. Many
police agencies have begun using human relations
training (or T-groups, or sensitivity training,
or communications training), as attempts to
increase the sensitivity and effectiveness of
police officers within the department (Reddy
and Lansky, 1976) and/or to attempt to improve
communications between police and community
residents (Sprafkin, et al, 1973). Human
relations training within police agencies has
developed largely because of its utilization
in other agencies in relationship to the
resolution of immediate internal and external
problems. With the explosion of social
problems (racial, juvenile, anti-war demon-
strations, etc.), the social scientist with
human relations skills has been incorporated

in police activities as a means of opening
communication between groups. However, the
effectiveness of group leaders in this area is
extremely dependent upon their understanding of
the parties involved, the purpose of the goals
of the group, and the nature of the organization
of the group.

Often such groups are organized on an
involuntary or paid basis rather than in
response to participant need and interest, and
consequently a great deal of time and energy
is spent trying to get the group to function.
To avoid this situation the group leader should
initiate group discussion by exploring why he
or she is involved in the training program,
thereby establishing what other participants'
expectancies are and utilize this vehicle to
stimulate the group to establish goals and
objectives congruent with its needs.

As indicated earlier, many of these groups
are initiated because of some immediate internal
or external problem.   Therefore, the focus of
such groups should be problem-centered, rather
than process-centered. This provides immediate
clarity for participants in terms of understanding
concretely the techniques of a group leader.
Communication styles, attitudes, and problem
solving orientation should be tied directly to
the context of the problem being discussed and
not presented abstractly. While individual
growth should be an intended goal, the primary
focus should be to resolve concrete problems
that exist within the police department, and
between police officers and other segments
of the community.

Finally, the organization of the group
should be determined by the issues involved
and not by arbitrary standards of availability,
reward or punishment.

5) *Community Relations*   Social
scientists working in this area need to
carefully assess the *real* purpose of their
work. Too often, community relations programs
are merely superficial public relations attempts
to convey a positive image of the police to the
community. Frequently, one finds that officers
are assigned to the community relations section
of a police department because they have not
been effective inother areas of police work,
and the work of these divisions is usually
conducted in relative isolation from the major
operations of the police agency.

Community relations consultation is a
viable role for social scientists to play in
law enforcement agencies because it is a
function that could serve to defuse problems
before they develop into explosive situations.
The skills of a social scientist could be
utilized to assist the police department and
community groups to develop and evaluate
programs which relate directly to the expressed
needs of a community.

The skills of community relations become
extremely important when one considers the fact
that approximatly 85 per cent of all police
work is not related to criminality but rather
to a variety of services. The acceptance of
a police officer's role in a community is
often directly related to the historical
relationship between that community and the
police department. It is in the nonlaw
enforcement areas, even more than in the direct
discharge of legal duties that the police
agency may benefit from community relations
assistance provided by scientists. The
social scientists role would be to impart
interpersonal skills to officers and to work
with police agencies in order to develop and
evaluate programs in conjunction with
community groups.

7) *Administrative Consultant* The
major roles of social scientists as consultants
to police agencies have been primarily defined
by situational problems, which has invariably
led to the performance of specific tasks in
relation to these problems. In these instances,
consultants have usually worked directly with
line personnel. Very little effort has been
directed toward working with the executive
personnel of law enforcment agencies as an
administrative consultant (Schwartz and Liebman,
1972). Since we are now referring to policy
and systemic consultation rather than specific
problem areas, the problem becomes one of
availability of vehicles for entering into
the administrative consultation relationships
with chiefs, whom heretofore have not perceived
a need in this area. Seeking outside help is
often perceived as an admission of inadequacy
or of administrative failure. Therefore,
police executive are reluctant to solicit
resources outside of the department.

As Schwartz and Liebman (1972) have noted,
there are a variety of roles that a consultant
can play at the administrative level, including
giving suggestions, questioning policies and
programs, providing assistance in planning,
listening actively and offering support to
police administrators who are confronted with
enormous pressures and frustration. Schwartz
and Liebman also caution the potential
administrative consultant to avoid creating
situations in which one's role becomes muddled
and confused (e.g., serving as an unintentional
conveyor of information between divisions of
the same police department).

For the individual interested in serving
as a consultant with a police agency, there
appear to be a wide selection of possible roles
to choose from. The selection of any given
role is a relative matter. There is no

"best" role. In any particular situation, the role choice should be made primarily on the basis of the expressed needs of the particular police department and the specific skills and experiences of the consultant. When there is a choice to be made between two comparable functions, the consultant should opt for the one which will most likely result in an immediate tangible benefit for the department. Regardless of which role one chooses, the social scientist should carefully monitor the ongoing process of developing a consultative relationship, utilizing a set of critical guidelines such as the six principles of Lippitt (1962) offered earlier in this chapter. The use of a guiding model will enable the consultant and the police agency to adapt their relationship as it develops, rather than allow it to remain on a single course which may not be serving the needs of the agency or the best interest of the consultant.

REFERENCES

1. Bard, M. *Training police as specialists in family crisis intervention*. U.S. Government Printing Office, Washington, D. C., 1970.

2. Caplan, G. *Principles of Preventive Psychiatry*. New York: Basic Books, 1964.

3. Lippitt. Dimensions of the consultant's job. In W. G. Benni, K. D. Benne, and R. Chen (Eds.), *The Planning of change: Readings in the Applied Behavioral Sciences*. New York: Holt, Rinehart & Winston, 1962, pp. 156-162.

4. Oglesby, S.,Sprafkin, R., Cohen, R. and Angelini, D. An evaluation of the Effects on citizen attitudes of the crime control team experiment. Paper presented at the *82nd Annual Convention of the American Psychological Association*, New Orleans, September, 1974.

5. Pepinsky, H. E. Goal definition for police patrolmen. In R. Cohen, R. Sprafkin, S. Oglesby, W. Claiborn (Eds.), *Working with Police Agencies*. New York: Behavioral Publications, 1975.

6. Phelps, L., Schwartz, J. A. and Liebman, D. A.

Training an entire partrol division in domestic crisis intervention *Police Chief,* 1970.

7. Reddy, W. B. and Lansky, L. M. Nothing but the facts--and some observations on norms and values: The history of a consultation with a metropolitan police division. In *Journal of Social Issues,* Vol. 30. (Also in R. Cohen, et al. (Eds.)

8. Schwartz, J. A. and Liebman, D.A. Mental health roles in law enforcement consultation. Paper presented at *Second Annual Symposium on Current Issues in Community Psychology: Working with Police Agencies,* Syracuse, New York, May, 1972.

9. Sprafkin, R.P., Angelini, D., Himmelsbach, J., Yorke, R. and Riordan, N. An evaluation of a human relations training program for police and community residents. Paper presented at the *Annual Convention of the Eastern Psychological Association,* Washington, D. C., May, 1973.

3. GOAL DEFINITION FOR POLICE PATROLMEN

Harold E. Pepinsky

The authors of the previous chapter suggest that there are a variety of legitimate consultative roles which social scientists may serve with a police agency. The current chapter has been selected because it emphasizes a particular type of consultation that logically should take precedence over the other services in terms of time sequence. Harold E. Pepinsky discusses the importance of facilitating the process of goal definition for police agencies. He stresses the need to establish clear cut objectives for police officers in order to enable them to work effectively. Pepinsky believes that the social scientist cannot define these goals for the police, but must facilitate the process of having police and citizens work actively together to discover mutually agreed upon goals.

One of the significant implications of Pepinsky's paper is that the social scientist needs to assist police officials in establishing basic priorities and stated objectives before attempting to help in areas of training or program development. Unless the police agency has determined what functions it wants to perform, it will probably be futile for the consultant to attempt to enhance skills and programs related to how the work will be performed.

INTRODUCTION

Underlying most discussions of "working with police" is an assumption that the "correct" goals of police work are known and clear. The police may then be criticized for failure to follow their mandate (Milner, 1971), or else action is proposed to make the goals more salient to the police than they now appear to be (Brown, 1973). However, extended observation of routine police patrol in a "high-crime area" in Minneapolis renders the assumption problematic (Pepinsky, 1972). Either goals are unstated or they are stated in a way that makes their fulfillment on the street impracticable.

These findings will be discussed in some detail in the next section of the chapter. The findings suggest that arriving at *a priori* goals for police patrolmen is a self-defeating undertaking. Though formal organizational theory generally sets goal definition as a precondition for organizational effectiveness, the conceptualization does not in itself solve the problem of goal definition for the police and their communities. As discussed in the third section of the chapter, the police and the community they are to serve function as an integral unit. The goals should therefore be those of police - citizen organizations. And since what is needed and what is practicable can be expected to vary from community to community, the sets of goals must vary accordingly. The police and citizens rather than outside consultants are in the best position to develop realistic goals for themselves. *The social-scientist-consultant can best define the procedure for police-citizen definition of goals, rather than attempting to specify what the substance of the goals should turn out to be.* The recommendation in the third section of the chapter is therefore of a procedure for each community to follow in defining its goals. In initiating structure for the police rather than defining the *substance* of goals for them, the effort here focuses of a definition of *procedure* for goal setting.

THE MINNEAPOLIS FINDINGS

The Minneapolis study was designed principally to determine how patrolmen decide whether officially to report offenses in response to calls from the police dispatcher. This author himself rode with the patrolmen in one Minneapolis precinct for 600 hours, during which time he not only gathered data on offense reporting, but observed the full range of patrol activities. There was a variety of kinds of activities in which the police engaged during the Minneapolis study. A basic distinction is useful in this description. In the terms of Reiss (1971, pp.64), this distinction is between *proactive* and *reactive* patrol activity. When patrolmen respond to a situation they discover themselves, the response is called *proactive*. When they respond to a call from the police dispatcher, the response is called *reactive*.

Most of the observed proactive responses of the police were in the area of traffic regulation. In this category, a number of drivers were stopped after the drivers were seen to have violated one or more traffic laws, such as by failing to stop for a red light or by driving a car with faulty equipment. A lesser but still substantial number of drivers were stopped merely out of suspicion that they were driving while intoxicated, or driving under a suspended or revoked license, or had outstanding arrest warrants for failure to pay traffic fines. Usually, these latter drivers were minority groups members and invariably the drivers were in older model, often dilapidated cars. Though less than 50 per cent, the likelihood of these drivers' being violators was great enough to reinforce a self-fulfilling prophecy that special suspicion of minority group drivers of older model cars was legitimate.

Traffic enforcement thus becomes the first evidence in support of a general rule. Unless patrolmen view the actual commission of an offense, proactive interrogation and investigation of suspects if more likely than not to be unwarranted. Catching offenders before they are known to have committed crimes tends to be a frustrating and fruitless effort; in this respect, the goal of crime prevention is unrealistic. Indeed, it often promotes citizen resentment of the police and on occasion leads to physical altercations between citizens and police.

The rule applies more strongly to proactive police activities other than traffic regulation. Seldom did the police see other offenses being committed without responding to a call. In the more than 600 hours of observation, the observer saw only one such case. Burglars were seen leaving a house with stolen goods. In this instance the observer happened to be in a squad called to back up the patrolmen who discovered the offense.

On numerous other occasions, the patrolmen questioned suspicious--looking citizens, including those parked in alleys, running across yards, walking darkened streets, or gathered in groups, especially at night. Not once did these investigations uncover offenses or lead to arrests. The chance of a squad car happening to be in the right place at the right moment to witness an offense such as a burglary or a robbery even in an area of a few square blocks is miniscule, "Adam 12" to the contrary notwithstanding. Proactive patrol activity cannot be an effective instrument of crime prevention, and the police should be relieved of the burden of trying to accomplish the task.

During a sample of 40 eight-hour patrols, the police made a total of six arrests, each in response to one of the 373 calls they received

from the dispatcher. Five of the six arrests
were on outstanding warrants; one was for disorder-
ly conduct. This excludes a number of traffic
arrests. In reactive police patrol work, then,
arrest was seldom used as a tool of law enforcement
Outside of traffic enforcement, "bringing offenders
to justice" did not prove to be a realistic goal
of police patrol either. (Note that the goal
might still be realistic for specialized police
units such as the detective, insofar as findings
apply to patrolmen only.)

It is true that patrolmen play a substantial
role in the initiation of investigation that can
later lead to arrest. They do this by filing
offense reports and memoranda to specialized units.

Memoranda are rarely used. Twice in the
study, memoranda were sent to the juvenile division,
and once to the narcotics division. Rarely did
the patrolmen uncover information useful to law
enforcement unless they filed offense reports.

In the offense report, patrolmen provide
information that is vital to police work in two
ways. Not only does it provide information basic
to criminal investigations, but it provides the
official data about what kinds of crimes are
occurring when and where. Though students of
victim-reporting (Ennis, 1967) and of self-
reporting (Williams and Gold, 1972) point to the
inadequacies of official data, the official data
still provide important clues as to the nature of
law enforcement efforts the police are asked to
make.

The taking of offense reports took a major
portion of the patrolmen's time. In 45 calls to
traffic offenses, the patrolmen effectively
reported offenses by writing traffic tags in 11
cases. Of the other 328 calls, the patrolmen
reported offenses in 86 of them. Allowing for
the nine cases in which multiple reports were

filed, these included eight robbery and purse
snatching reports, twenty-nine theft reports,
four assault reports, 11 damage to property
(vandalism) reports, three sex offense reports,
two more traffic tags and four reports of other
minor violations of city ordinances, including,
for example, glue - sniffing. A bias check
showed the percentages of various types of offense
reports in the sample to be comparable to the
overall percentages in the precinct during the
observation period.

The study showed that the police exercised
discretion in calls to traffic offenses (45), to
sex offenses (eight), and to assaults (14). Of
the 207 calls in which the dispatcher named no
offense in the call, the police were recorded to
have reported an offense on only four occasions.
One of these four was probably miscoded by the
observer and was actually a call to check a theft.
Another was a call to "check a car," which turned
out to be blocking a driveway and was tagged and
towed. A third was one in which a citizen started
screaming at the police and was arrested for
distrubing the peace. The last was one in which
the police dispatched to check "kids disturbing,"
found children sniffing paint in violation of a
city ordinance and took them into custody.

The police were apparently unprepared to
report offenses in response to calls to attempted
offenses (two) or to victimless crimes, here,
possession of marijuana (one). Of the 96
remaining calls to other offenses, the police
failed to report offenses in only 21 cases. In
eight of these 21, the patrolman saw no complainant, in three they did not believe the complainant
stated any offense, in two the complainant knew
the suspect, in one the complainant requested
that no report be made, in one the complainant
invited vandalism in an attempted auto theft
by violating the law himself (leaving the keys
in his ignition), and in one burglary call, only

75 cents was missing and was deemed too minor
to bother with.

On the other hand, in calls in which no
offenses were named, complainants' allegations
would have supported offense reports in at least
three cases for aggravated assault, seven cases
for simple assault causing injury, four cases of
assault causing no injury, two cases for grand
theft, five cases for damage to property and one
case for illegal use of a firearm. The handling
of damage to property reports rounds out the
picture. The patrolmen filed reports in all but
one of the 11 cases in which they were dispatched
to check damage to property, the exception being
the case in which the complainant had left keys in
the ignition. The two calls to attempted offenses
were to attempted burglaries. Though property
damage had occurred in both cases, the police
reported neither offense.

The pattern is clear. In the overwhelming
number of reactive responses in which the patrolmen
find complainants, the category of the call
determined whether an offense is reported. The
police exercised significant discretion only in
calls to check traffic offenses, sex offenses and
assaults. Otherwise, the decision as to whether
to report an offense, if made over the phone without
dispatching patrolmen to the scene, would be
practically the same as that made by the patrolmen.

This leads to the question of whether sending
the patrolmen to almost 100 of the 373 calls to
report offenses was simply a waste of time. In a
relatively few of these cases, the dispatcher would
have had reason to send the patrolmen to check for
an offense in progress, to help someone in physical
or mental distress, to clarify confusing information
or to gather evidence. But dispatch to about a
fourth of all calls in the sample, merely to perform the clerical task of making out offense
reports, was a waste of manpower and time.

It did not even serve to reassure complainants, who tended instead to be frustrated that the patrolmen came only to take information and could promise no results. It is more likely that a complainant would be reassured by being informed that a squad car to take any possible action on information received than by facing a pair of uninformed stenographers.

Hence, in the vast majority of cases excepting traffic regulation, the goal of law enforcement was unreasonable and aggravating for patrolmen to be expected to fulfill. It should be emphasized that the patrolmen did not fail to do a conscientious job of offense reporting. The unreasonability of the job was in expecting that the patrolmen could do anything important in the job. No amount of judiciously used skill could have discerned the lying complainant from the truthful, for example. The ideal of the assignment was unobtainable, and the task became meaningless. There remains a great residuum of reactive patrol activity, responding to what is euphemistically termed "service calls." Obvious service was performed in the 12 cases in which the police conveyed sick and injured citizens to the hospital. Nor can the value of such services as looking for lost children and helping people into locked homes and cars be discounted.

However, most "service calls" involve trying to settle disputes between parties. The 16 calls to "domestics"- fights within families - are the most obviously troubling example. The most the patrolmen accomplished was to separate the feuding parties temporarily. Generally, the resentment of the parties was displaced onto the patrolmen. Special training the patrolmen received in handling "domestics" focused on how the police could withdraw and do as little as possible, for it was agreed that there was little else the police could do without causing more trouble than they found. In other categories of this kind of call, such as neighbor

disputes, landlord-tenant conflicts, and loud
music complaints, the situations were similarly
irresolvable in almost every instance. Instead
of getting affirmation that they were fulfilling
a goal of service, the patrolmen tended to
receive damnation.

The circumstances of the Minneapolis patrolmen
are sad not, as so many suggest, because the
patrolmen did not want to perform their duties, but
because for the most part they were not given duties
that could demonstrably be ably performed. Most
of the patrolmen were young enough not to have
become cynical, and made sincere attempts to help
citizens where they could do so. This situation
in Minneapolis is probably not atypical, and
presents a challenge to a society that expects
meaningful service from the police. That challenge
is to develop realistic goals that competent and
willing policemen can fulfill.

THE ACCOMPLISHMENT OF GOAL DEFINITION

No theorist of formal organizations would
take exception to the proposition that definition
of organizational goals is a precondition to
organizational effectiveness. Quite simply, one
needs to know *what* is to be accomplished by members
of an organization before one can assess the
significance of *whether* something is to be
accomplished.

Somehow, though, theorists of formal
organizations generally tend to make goal
definition seem to be rather a mythical process.
The social scientist studying an organization
typically gives the impression either (a) that he
need only "find" existing authoritative goals,
(b) that he can choose goals and the organization
will readily subscribe to them or (c) that he can
merely confront leaders of an organization with a
need to define goals and that workable goals will
be forthcoming. The police provide a case in

point that goal definition may not so easily be
accomplished. The lack of viable goals for police
patrolmen reflects the facts (a) that the goals
do not exist, (b) that numerous social scientific
commentators and consultants have been unable to
define the goals for the patrolmen and (c) that
police administrators have proved incapable of
goal definition for their patrolmen employees.

There is no dearth of abstract goals given
to patrolmen to guide their work. The problem is
that the abstract goals become ambiguous, unrealistic or mutually contradictory when applied to concrete
cases. For instance, as alluded to above, while the
Minneapolis study was being conducted, a team of
psychologists were carrying out a program to train
patrolmen how to respond to calls involving domestic
disputes. When the psychologists began to learn the
details of actual cases faced by the patrolmen, the
psychologists quickly came to despair of meeting
the challenge of goal definition. Their solution
was to tell the patrolmen there was practically
nothing worthwhile they could accomplish and
therefore that the patrolmen had best seek to leave
the domestic disputants as soon after arriving as
possible. The message to the patrolmen was that
they could do harm but no good, and that they had
better do nothing but watch out for their personal
safety and extricate themselves as quickly as they
could from an untenable situation.

A lesson of experience in working with police
is that instead of attempting to define goals for
patrolmen and their citizen - clientele, the
patrolmen and their clients will have to be equipped
to define goals for themselves. The task before
the social - scientist - consultant is not that of
defining the substance of patrolmens' goals, but to
define a procedure by which goals can be developed
and revised by those who must meet them. Thus,
the procedure for arriving at goal definition
rather than the substance of goals themselves
will be discussed here.

There are three important considerations to bear in mind in establishing a procedure for goal definition for patrolmen. First, what citizen - clients do is as important to the meeting of a goal as is what the patrolmen do themselves. This is generally expressed by patrolmen in terms of a need for citizen cooperation. For example, if one goal is for patrolmen to catch burglars in a neighborhood, they can hardly do so without citizens watching out for burglars and calling for assistance. Or if another goal is to help spouses not to fight, the spouses have to want the help to be given.

Second, even within one precinct, the needs and therefore the goals for patrol service vary considerably from one district to the next, and even among parts of one district. For example, there might be a number of drunks on the sidewalk on only a couple of blocks of one street in a precinct. Therefore, the procedure should allow for patrolmen assigned to differenct areas to arrive at different sets of goals.

Third, the problems and hence the appropriate goals may change in a given area from time to time, and goals once thought viable may later prove to be nonviable. For example, the children in one neighborhood may perform considerable vandalism in the summer but not in the winter. Therefore, the procedure for goal definition must be permanent and continuous; it must allow for reassessment of existing goals.

These considerations dictate that a procedure be established for patrolmen in each district to meet repeatedly with a variety of groups of citizens residing and doing business there. The question then arises as to how these meetings are to be organized.

The first problem is to locate groups of citizens and bring them to meetings. Initially, at least, it would probably be overly ambitious to create groups especially for the purpose of meeting with patrolmen. The history of community organization has mostly been one of frustration over stimulating citizen participation in community action. It is better to risk malapportionment of citizen representation in goal definition for patrolmen than it is to risk non-representation, and so active, established groups, such as churches, schools, chambers of commerce and political committees, should be approached to meet with patrolmen.

Most urban police departments today have community relations units. Typically, members of these units are speech-makers. Where such units exist, their members can serve as coordinators for arranging the patrolmen-citizen meetings. Where such units do not exist, they should be established for coordination purposes. Community relations officers' primary responsibilities would be to locate established citizen groups, contact their leaders, set up times and places for the meetings and serve as informal chairmen at the meetings.

In police departments that have not already done so, manpower would need to be allocated so that two patrol units are on duty at any one time in each district. The Model City Precinct in Minneapolis provides an example of how this can be done. In each district, there were three basic shifts of eight hours apiece (not counting an extra shift to cover heavy activity in the early evening hours). Three secondary shifts overlapped the three basic ones. Thus, the early day watch began at 7:00 a.m., the late watch at 10:00 a.m. The early middle watch began at 3:00 p.m., the late middle watch at 6:00 p.m. The early dog watch began at 11:00 p.m., the late dog watch at 2:00 a.m. The car on early day watch was on primary status from 7:00 - 11:00 a.m. to 3:00 p.m., and so on. Thus, each car on regular patrol had primary responsibility for answering calls for four house, and back-up responsibility for the other four. If these cars were unable to handle emergency calls, a car was dispatched from a neighboring district.

In this situation, the back-up patrolman or patrolmen could have been out of service at any time without seriously impairing the capability for handling calls in any given district. Meetings could easily be scheduled for back-up patrolmen to attend meetings with citizens for a couple of hours. The benefits of potentially improved service from goal definition with citizens should outweigh the costs of taking back-up patrolmen off the streets.

With citizens and back-up district patrolmen in attendance at the meetings, the community relations officers would introduce discussion with one short question: "What can the patrolmen do for you citizens, and what can the citizen do for you patrolmen?" Perhaps members of a church could provide a place for patrolmen to bring public drunks for the night. Perhaps patrolmen could try to obtain portable radio units for citizen street patrols to call in police assistance. Perhaps citizens could be encouraged to get their neighbors to watch carefully for signs of burglars while they were away. Perhaps a committee of citizens and patrolmen could develop lists of referral services for the patrolmen to use in response to various kinds of crises.

Out of the meetings, the patrolmen and the citizens should develop a sense of what they could reasonably expect from one another, and discuss how best to do what was expected. As patrolmen and citizens encounter problems with one another, they could raise the problems in the meetings with a view to resolution.

For the patrolmen-citizen goal definition process to be effective, it would have to be reflected in the reward structure of the police department. Thus, the community relations officers, would be given responsibility for distilling criteria of patrol performance to correspond to the expectations of patrolmen coming from the

meetings. When a community relations officer
in a district could arrive at a set of operational
criteria which all of the patrolmen in the district
and the leaders of participating groups signed, the
criteria would be placed in the personnel file of
each district patrolman. The sergeant or sergeants
in the district would then be given primary
responsibility for making periodic evaluations
of the patrolmen, *in terms of the agreed-upon
criteria only*. Hence, for example, unless the
patrolmen and citizens agreed that patrolmen
should make arrests for particular offenses, records
of arrests for those offenses would *not* be
included in the patrolmen's files. When a civil
service group rated a patrolman's work and scored
it on a promotional examination, the score would
be based on the criteria that peculiarly arose
from the police-citizen interaction in one district.
If any group or any patrolman petitioned the
community relations officer for a revision of the
criteria, the community relations officer would
be obliged to circulate the revision for possible
approval and subsequent use.

Under the premise, then, that there is a need
to define police patrolmen's goals for their work,
this is a proposal not of what the goals should
be but of how they should be obtained.

CONCLUSION

Chambliss and Seidman (1971, pp. 261-270) have
correctly observed that police work is generally
characterized by goal displacement. The police
try to concoct appearances that they are meeting
goals ostensibly given them by society without
actually working to meet the goals. However, it
is not fair to conclude, as do Chambliss and
Seidman, that the goal displacement is simply a
cynical abuse of power -- an effort by police to
get away with whatever they can.

Instead, observations of police patrolmen

in Minneapolis support the proposition that
police sincerely want to meet goals of service
to their communities, but have no viable goals
to meet. Police cynicism can result from the
lack of goals, to be sure. But it would be a
mistake to believe that the police can be
restrained from acting out of cynicism merely
by closer surveillance and imposition of
harsher sanctions. To begin with, the police
must be given meaningful goals to fulfill.

No distant observer can list these goals
for the police. Those who must fulfill the
goals, i.e., the police and the citizens with
whom they interact, must create those goals for
themselves. The social scientist as consultant
has a key role to play in this effort, but not
a role he is often called upon to play. It is
not for the consultant to try to decide what
police patrolmen should be doing on the street,
for he can do this with marginal effectiveness
at best. The consultant can best play the role
of social organizer or animator, pointing out
the need for goal definition procedures, and
helping the police to establish those procedures
and accompanying reward structures. This in
itself would represent a significant step
toward more effective police patrol work.

REFERENCES

1. Brown, W. P.   A cybernetic conceptualization of the police task.   (unpublished paper).

2. Chambliss, W. J., Seidman, R. B.   *Law, Order and Power*.   Reading, Mass.:   Addison-Wesley Publishing Co., 1971.

3. Ennis, R. H.   Crime, victims and the police.   *Trans-Action* 4 (7) 36-44, 1967.

4. Milner, N. A.   *The Court and Local Law Enforcement: The Impact of Miranda*.   Beverly Hills: Sage Publications, 1971.

5. Pepinsky, H. E.   Police decisions to report offenses.   Dissertation prepared at University of Pennsylvania, 1972.

6. Reiss, A. J., Jr.   *The Police and the Public*.   New Haven: Yale University Press, 1971.

7. Williams, J. R., and Gold, M.   From delinquent behavior to official delinquency.   *Social Problems,* 20:   209-229, 1972.

4. CONSEQUENCES OF COOPERATION BETWEEN POLICE
    AND MENTAL HEALTH SERVICES:
    ISSUES AND SOME SOLUTIONS

Joseph T. Himmelsbach

*Joseph Himmelsbach's work with the police
has been somewhat unique. While most practitioners
who work with police agencies have limited contact
with the officers, either in class or through a
periodic consultation, Himmelsbach's crisis
evaluation work brought him and his team into
continuous onsite contact with law enforcement
officers. The intensive, action-oriented relationship that evolved between these mental health
workers, and the police, engendered many conflicts
and some resolutions.*

*In this paper, the author describes some of
the issues he has confronted in his work with the
police. Drawing primarily on direct personal
experience, he enumerates the obstacles which may
impede the development of an effective working
relationship with the police, and then proposes
some possible methods for reducing these obstacles.*

*One of the major themes of this paper is
that social science practitioners need to deal
openly and directly with value and orientation
issues when entering into a relationship with a
police agency. It may not be possible to achieve
a consensus of opinion in all areas, but if
practitioners and police are able to clarify*

their own basic attitudes and roles,
communicate openly with each other about their
perceptions, and arrange to observe, first hand,
the work each performs, then the possibility
of establishing a viable working relationship
will be greatly enhanced.

Much has been written concerning the inter-
relatedness of police duties and community mental
health work. Liberman (1969) reports that 50
per cent of all first contacts to mental hospitals
are referred by police. Whittington (1971) found
that in many communities the police are the gate
keepers for most social services. This interface,
at times, results in difficulties because of the
difference in style, philosophy, methods and
goals of the two groups.

We are faced with a dilemma. The reality
of laws, circumstances, expectancies and traditions
would suggest a harmonious working relationship.
However, when attempts are made at police -
mental health service cooperation, the process is
rarely smooth. Some examples from this author's
experience of the types of difficulties encountered are as follows: (1) police resistance to
engage in any behavior which simulates "social
work" (2) the mental health worker's refusal or
inability to understand how a police service
operates (3) the loss of the mental health
worker's"professional identity" when he becomes
to enmeshed in police activities(i.e. becoming a
"deputy cop")(4) police discomfort with dealing
with mental health professionals ("shrinks").
In spite of these problems, cooperative
programs between the two groups are developing
throughout the country. These cooperative ventures
involve joint decision making. Because of the
myriad forces operating in these decisions,
crises often occur when conflicts emerge. The
crisis usually revolves around which group's
decision will be implemented.

The crisis can be resolved in a negative or positive fashion. An example of the negative result would be having a mental health worker make a decision about a patient solely on the input of relevant police variables. From the police view, a negative outcome would consist of a loss of their unique natural talent or expertise in dealing with human problems in deference to the "expert's input." A positive outcome would include both groups functioning in their defined capacity, with the goal being the optimum outcome for the individual in question.

The purpose of this chapter is threefold: first, it is a plea to these groups to be cautious in their cooperative undertakings; second, it is an attempt to outline some potential porblem areas which can aggravate the difficulty, and third, it offers some solutions to reduce the probability of these problems occurring.

The information which is presented here was gathered from personal experiences in working with the police over a two-year period. Our working with the police was not the result of a project grant but rather the result of the harsh necessity of developing a crisis intervention program to serve persons considered dangerously mentally ill. This program, initiated by the local mental health department, was responsible for assisting the police evaluate persons whom the police felt were "mentally ill and dangerous" according to the statutes of the State Mental Hygiene Law. It was the development of this program which resulted in the surfacing of some pre-existing crucial differences between police and mental health workers.

The ideas presented have been generated from the author's participant observation in the program. Because of the sensitive nature of the program the gathering of "objective"data on police-mental health worker relations was not possible.

ISSUES IMPEDING COOPERATION BETWEEN POLICE AND
MENTAL HEALTH WORKERS

Three general areas of potential conflict
emerged from reflection on the program. These
areas are: legal issues, program goals, and values
and attitudes. Problems in cooperative efforts
could be due to any one or any combination of areas.

Legal Conflicts In most of the 50 states,
both the police and the mental health authorities
are legitimate social control agents. However,
the police in all cases have more extensive legal
power and can be involved in many more situations
of legal intervention than can the mental health
worker (Bittner, 1967). Social control via mental
health services is real although usually it is
less obvious and circumscribed. For example,
every peace officer has the power to arrest an
individual, however, in the mental health area
only physicians can legally commit people.

Most police are aware of the physician's
power to commit and detain. They view this as a
legitimate function of mental health professionals.
The conflict arises when the police insist that
the mental health people use *their* legal authority
as the police utilize their own. That is, mental
health workers should detain people quickly,
based on minimal "probable cause" information.
Also, at times, the police feel that mental health
services should utilize the detention process for
purposes other than explicit mental health intervention. (For example, to commit an elderly, possibly
organic, person who refuses to take a bath, not
because he is dangerous but rather to insure that
he receives some proper hygienic treatment.) The
police may become very upset when the mental
health worker refuses to respond immediately to
their request for detention. Although most
mental hygiene law committal statutes are cumber-
some, by design, to prevent such precipitous
decisions.

Apparently, this issue is mainly a function of the structure of the laws. It holds out the mental health worker as an ally to the police, but in practical terms, he is a weak ally at best. This creates confusion, distrust and anger within the police, since it is perceived by them as a refusal on the part of the mental health services to do their fair share.

Program Conflicts This area relates to the legitimate, oftentimes legally mandated goals of a particular organization. It includes the overt statements about their program goals, the operations of their service and the manner in which the service is provided.

In any cooperative effort between the police and mental health workers, these areas should be examined extensively. It is usually easier to evolve a discussion in this area, rather than in the covert area of values and attitudes. The program issues are more overt, less threatening and may be open to compromise or increased understanding.

The usual police program is to provide a service that is responsive to the needs of the entire community. The police are paid to maintain the laws, standards and, in some cases, the morality of the community. In order to accomplish this, they are given the authority by the community to protect community members from those "deviants" who would threaten their laws, standards and morality. They have sworn to uphold the laws of the community and defend the community against all attacks on these laws. Police agencies usually make decisions on the basis of the "greater good" or the "rights of others" concepts.

On the other hand, most mental health professionals, from the orthodox analyst to the community psychologist, place the needs of their "patient" first. Their decisions are usually responsive to the needs of the individual who is presenting the problem. Instead of defending the community as it exists, they may ask it to change or to become more tolerant in order to insure the client's survival.

This dichotomy is not absolute. However, the operating principles which are displayed by either group reflect this basic difference. In viewing a similar situation, the police officer and mental health worker may reach a different decision based on these different principles. These principles are operating when the police are faced with a dangerous or potentially dangerous situation and base their decision on public safety. In a similar manner, the mental health worker would probably base his decision, in the same situation, on the individual's ability to behave in a responsible, adult fashion.

Our service was involved in numerous situations where this difference became an issue. In a typical case the following call was received from the police: A woman in her late 20's contacted the police about a man who refused to leave her apartment. She had dated this man at one time; he came to see her and refused to leave. The police officer arrived at the scene and found the man staunchly refusing to leave, acting in a somewhat "irrational" manner (i.e., insisting that the girl really loved him) but not threatening or dangerous in any way. Naturally, the woman wanted him removed from her apartment.

In the officer's opinion, the man was not really a "criminal" but was having problems and could probably benefit from psychiatric care. The policeman contacted our mobile evaluation service. He hoped that we would suggest hospitalization, either voluntary or involuntary, thus removing the man from the situation as well as providing "help."

Our evaluation, however, was not to the
officer's satisfaction. Our people talked to
the individual and determined that he was not
psychotic, that he knew he was in this girl's
apartment and that he could possibly be arrested
for trespassing. Essentially, he was aware of
his situation and responsible for his actions.
We offered him the option of voluntary psycho-
therapy and he refused. We then informed the
police officer that we could not provide any
other service.

Naturally, the officer became upset at
this point. He was hoping for a quick, efficient
resolution of the problem which he felt would be
in everyone's best interest. He did not receive
that from the mental health workers. He could
not leave the situation and allow the man to
remain. His only alternative was to begin the
process of having the woman swear out a formal
complaint (trespassing is a misdeameanor) and
arrest the individual. His feelings were that
this would be unfair since the man "obviously
had problems" and was not the "criminal type."

It is with these situations that a conflict
becomes most apparent. The police officer is
concerned about the safety of others, the family
for example, but the individual in question has
yet to break the law. He appears quite threatening, but has not done anything which would
warrant an arrest. The police officer hopes that
his ally in social control, the mental health
worker, would also be responsive to the issue of
potential harm. Instead, he receives a report
which indicates that the person is responsible
for his actions. That is all. Here begins the
strain in cooperation.

Both the police and mental health worker
agree that the individual may have "problems".
However, the police are reticent to utilize
legal power and satisfy their stated mandate

of public safety. Concurrently, the mental
health workers refuse to undertake an intervention which would hospitalize the individual.

If this example were to be expanded,
other program differences which have the potential
for interfering with police - mental health
cooperation would become apparent. Consider the
situation wherein a potential assault was due
to a family dispute or a marital fight. In this
crisis situation, a police officer and a mental
health worker would again be operating out of
two different and distinct styles.

In the training bulletin of a large East
Coast police department, under guidelines for
handling family disputes, police are instructed
to "Stop the direct, verbal confrontation of
disputants." Following this, as soon as possible,
they are instructed to "restore order and control
the situation" (Police Response to Family Disputes,
1969). Contrast this with the crisis techniques
as found in the psychological literature. There,
the emphasis is on free expression, catharsis,
confrontation and engendering autonomy rather
than dependence. If the police officer and
mental health worker were well trained in their
respective procedures, and, if both attempted
to resolve the family conflict, *they* would need
a referee.

Other difficulties in the program emerge
from certain internal paradoxes of police and
mental health service. Specifically, the police
are frequently utilized as resources for mental
health problems in the street, yet they usually
have minimal training in the area of mental
health. Conversely, mental health professionals
are trained to deal with the problems of the
mentally ill but the majority of these professionals have minimal experience with the street
aspects of the problem. These two area, mental
health expertise and street expertise, ordinarily

do not come into conflict with each other.
However, the decisions resulting from this
expertise may be in conflict. The police officer,
in viewing a problem from his orientation, may
feel that he is being more realistic and pragmatic.
His decision to refer someone to the hospital may
not be based on the issue of his mental illness,
but rather on the fact that his behaving in a
certain fashion, in a certain neighborhood,
would result in his being mugged. This "street"
assessment and recommedation may run counter to
the decision based on a psychiatric evaluation
of an individual's "ego functioning".

These differences can be observed in any
police-mental health interaction. They are usually
the more overt, operating methods and rationales
upon which decisions are based.

There is another covert area of difference
which can contribute to the potential difficulties.
This covert category includes such things as
attitudes, values and personality differences.

*Values and Attitude Differences - Impeding
Cooperation* It has been this author's observation
(with some support in research literature), that
most police officers are action - oriented and
rely heavily on active measures to resolve conflicts.
They are trained to respond quickly and decisively.
They utilize their authority to control and direct
a situation (Rokeach, Miller and Snyder, 1971).
If appropriate, they employ their ultimate legal
power and arrest an individual.

This can be contrasted to the observed
behavioral style of mental health workers. Most
people in this profession appear to be cognitively oriented, unwilling to make fast decisions,
and usually unwilling to take immediate action
to resolve a problem. They may attempt to gently
"persuade" a person by communicating understanding
and empathic statements. This low--key approach

is in direct contrast to the police method of
quick action to achieve closure on a case
(Trojanowicz, 1971).

This difference can be illustrated by a
situation in which the author was involved. It
concerned the transporting of a middle-aged,
borderline psychotic female, from her apartment
to the local psychiatric facility. The purpose
of our involvement was to expedite the situation
for the police. Upon our arrival, we instructed
the police to remain outside the apartment while
we talked with the woman. Our approach was
essentially as outlined above. We attempted to
understand her predicament, build up her trust,
be emphatic and subtly cajole her into leaving
for the hospital.

This process had been underway for about
20--25 minutes when one of the waiting police
officers became impatient and decided to take
matters into his own hands. He strode into the
room, interrupted the conversation with, "Is
she ready to come, Doc?", while placing his hand
on the woman's shoulder. Before we had an
opportunity to respond, he was gently but forcefully steering the woman towards the door, all
the while keeping up a chatter of benign,
authoritarian statements, such as "Let's go,ma'am
....Just step this way....Here's your purse, take
it along". This woman, who was being resistive
to our pleadings, responded to the officer's
approach. She went right along with the officer
to the hospital. We went along for the ride,
our "expediting" skills apparently unnecessary.

This situation did not result in a conflict
occurring between the police and our service.
However, in a different setting with different
goals, the contrasting styles could cause some
acute difficulties. In this instance, we shared
a common goal, arranging for the woman's
transportation to the hospital. However, if

the situation involved evaluating the need for possible hospitalization, our behaviors would have been the more effective approach.

In the latter situation, the decision to transport an individual would have to be held in abeyance while enough information was collected in order that the appropriate course of action be taken. In these situations, a cautious, calm, empathic interview usually results in acquiring more useable information. The complex human situation that contributes to mental illness is not discerned by a curt, yes or no interrogation. A police officer who becomes impatient and decides that the individual was "crazy" (If she weren't crazy, why would they call the mental health services?) may force an inappropriate if not traumatic action. If this action were carried out, the consequences would be unsatisfactory for the mental health personnel as well as the police. The mental health staff would feel angry at being bullied, they would object to an unnecessary admission and would be upset with the decision maker. The police officer would also be dissatisfied. When this individual arrived at the hospital, he probably would not be admitted, nor would the officer receive any support from the mental health staff for his decision.

It appears that the action orientation of the police is enhanced by their cognitive view of the world. Most police officers either join the force with or develop the survival strategy of being cognitively direct and uncomplicated. This involves viewing the world in terms of black and white, good and bad, law and anarchy. This may be a necessary strategy for the police to assist their coping with multifaceted and complex problems. It is required that they "do it by the book" and not be concerned with all of the subtle nuances of any given case. If they were to consider these nuances, it could result in their becoming obsessive to the extent that no action would be taken.

It is the author's observation that this last statement is descriptive of many mental health professionals. These individuals tend to be cognitively oriented, complex, obsessive and non-impulsive. For example, mental health professionals rarely make statements about the certainty of an event occurring, but rather consider the proba-bilities of its occurrence. In collecting information about cases, they become involved in minute details about the presenting situation as well as about marital history, developmental processes, work history and social contacts. It is the mental health professional's style to include all of these facts in his decision making. Therefore, his usual course is to never make an absolute decision. The absence of this decision usually runs counter to the police officer's expectancies.

In our own dealings with police, we have noticed that common-sense, layman's ideas about mental illness were offered by them as rationale for their decisions about the mentally ill. For example, the police speak frequently of the violent or potentially violent mentally ill person. Prevention of this violence is one of their main issues in providing service to the mentally ill. If one attempts to explain the different facets of a situation which could lead to violence and the inappropriateness of such blanket decisions, the mental health worker is viewed as being naive.

In much the same fashion, middle management of the police department have described mentally ill individuals as either being "good" people or "bad" people. Their actions when involved with such a person are largely determined by this value judgment. These judgments are placed on different individuals for many different reasons. For example, if an immediate assessment shows that the person is a hard worker, married and takes care of his children, he is a "good" person and should be treated accordingly. If he is a drunkard who wastes his money and his family suffers, he is a "bad" person. This results in similar situations (e.g., family fight) having entirely different outcomes. Being the "good" person allows for more beneficient treatment. Once this characterization is made, decisions are based upon it without benefit of additional information.

Another example of the cognitively uncomplicated decision system comes from a statement made by a high - level administrator in the police department. In talking about an individual who had been agitated and potentially assaultive, he determined that this person had "broken one of his wires." The implication of this statement was that the simple job of the mental health worker was to mend the broken wire which would stop the agitation and would allow the man to be placed back in his home. When this person was released from the hospital it was incomprehensible to this officer that the man could again behave in the same "irrational" fashion.

This is not to imply that the average policeman does not have the capacity for complex cognition. The point is that the best strategy for him in responding to the demands of a multi-input system is to adopt the cognitively uncomplicated attitude. It is this adopted strategy which can run counter to the role of the mental health worker. This combined with the mental health workers' tendencies not to be certain about anything leads to poor results. The consequences are basic disagreements about dispositions of cases, police insecurity with mental health workers' decisions, and resulting frustration on the part of the mental health workers.

Finally, in this author's judgment, there appears to exist an internal attitudinal system which contributes to the anxiety of both the

police and mental health worker. This system is
based on the reactions to and use of authority.
In this author's opinion, a majority of police
have the characteristics of overt authoritarians
(Talbott and Talbott, 1971). They are rigid,
controlled, responsive to authority messages and
are cognitively simple. The system in which they
operate serves as a self selector as well as a
reinforcer of these behaviors.

When these individuals are placed in
situations where the problems are amorphous (i.e.,
mental illness) or when they have to deal with
mental health workers (i.e., "shrinks") they
become quite anxious. The former causes problems
because they are uncomfortable with the cognitive
style. The latter develops from their attitudes
about the role of mental health workers as well
as the "authoritarian" perception that mental
health workers have an ability to "discover" the
"real" reasons why people act the way they do.
Everything spoken by a police officer would be
utilized by the "shrink" to "psych him out."
These issues are compounded when the police
officer is "put down" by the mental health worker
since only the latter understands why people act
the way they do. A police officer's observation
that two men are fighting because they are angry
runs a poor second to the mental health workers'
observation that one man is "compensating for
his inadequate sexuality." This entire process
of encounter is usually an uncomfortable one for
the police.

For differenct reasons, the experience can
also be anxiety arousing for the mental health
worker. It became apparent to this author that
many mental health workers become anxious when they
come into contact with the "overt authority" as
personified by the police.

There are many possible suggestions as
to why this reaction may occur. One possibility

concerns the mental health worker's response to
the issue of power and authority; specifically,
his reaction to these attributes in others. It
is the author's contention that most mental
health workers are "latent" authoritarians.
They may have had feelings similar to the police
on how to deal with deviant individuals but for
some reason their behavior changed (Trojanowicz,
1971). However, they see in the police the
expression of those feelings which they are
attempting to curb or change. In cooperating
with the police on certain cases, the controls
on these feelings may be threatened and thus
the anxiety develops. If the mental health
worker has not fully resolved this issue for himself,he may find himself developing the "police
attitude" in his dealing with the mentally ill,
or he may become so anxious that his effectiveness
is lessened.

A complimentary situation exists when
mental health workers are forced to argue and
disagree with the police administration on issues.
If the mental health workers are "latent authoritarians" then they will have a very difficult time
confronting the "real" authority around issues.
This may also cause anxiety to develop since they
realize what they should do (i.e., disagree
strongly) but are unable to do so. The end result
is a self perpetuating anxiety loop. Given the
growth of this anxiety, the ability of the worker
to support his opinion is curtailed.

An example of this occurred in a top level
administration meeting between police and mental
health workers on the issue of the detention of
the mentally ill. During the meeting, feelings
were quite strong. Following the session, one
administrative psychiatrist expressed the feeling
that he was "afraid to do battle" with a Deputy
Chief. Objectively, there was no rationale for
for this feeling. An assumption could be made
that such encounters with authority were quite

uncomfortable for this psychiatrist.

This concludes the presentation of issues
which may impede the cooperation between police
and mental health services. The points presented
here were distilled from one service in one community
and while it is assumed that there is generalization
to other communitues in other locales, this has
not been determined.

SOME SOLUTIONS

The solutions which follow can not be
characterized as unique or creative. They have
been discussed in other papers for other reasons.
It is their application to these particular problems
which may be somewhat different.

1) The first suggestion is in response to
the issue of values and attitudes. Mental health
workers, particularly those working with police
agencies, should establish in their own mind, a
strong professional identity. This identity should
include such factors as their ethical stance, their
treatment philosophy, their attitudes about mental
illness and health as well as their philosophical
views of man. It is the author's opinion that many
mental health workers lack a strong sense of who
they are and what they want to accomplish in the
field of mental health. They move from insight to
insight, from fad to fad, new therapy to new
therapy, never really taking stock of themselves
and their own personal value system. It is the
examination and establishment of this personal
value system that will be the benchmark for their
decisions. Without such a system, their ability
to withstand the pressure of other opinions is
lessened.

2) The second suggestion relates to program
conflicts. Mental health workers should define
publicly their stance for others on the germane
issues of their service. If it is a drug agency

they should be clear about their feelings on the use of drugs; a crisis team should define its stance on community intervention or the indiscriminate use of hospitalization, etc. These positions should be backed up with facts, figures and research along with personal conviction.

3)   The third suggestion also relates to program issues. When the program is defined, it should be adhered to scrupulously; the program's goals and values remain stable. This is not to say that one cannot modify program content, but the goals and philosophy of any mental health program should not change with the vagaries of political pressure or convenience. This is a prime source for the contradictions which begin to emerge and can cause acute anxiety among the staff.

4)   The fourth suggestion refers to legal and program issues. Most mental health programs are usually covertly political and one should be aware of that. This is to the advantage of the politicians and those who are conversant with the political-legal game, but it is to the disadvantage of mental health workers who are likely to be extremely naive in the ways of politics. All too often, excellent programs have been discontinued by political decisions. This occurred not because they were ineffective, but because these political decisions lacked sufficient input from the mental health staff. In addition, mental health professionals usually do not expend any time developing "political clout." Any special program runs the risk of being discontinued. It is necessary for their survival that they develop this political support to respond to these conflicts.

5)   The next solution also relates to program issues. It concerns the education of the community agencies and residents about the mental health service. Definitions should be given to them as to what services are going to be provided

and what are not to be provided. Only in this
way can mental health services exert some control
over the quality and use of the service. It also
lessens the problem of ignorance surrounding aspects
of service which are unique or non-traditional.

6) The final suggestion is a general one.
It relates to any service that works with the
police. The police should be given an opportunity
to experience first hand the services which are
provided without their being officially involved.
This would contribute to their appreciation of
other staff judgments and recommendations. In
particular, they should observe the outcomes
of these judgments. In like manner, the mental
health workers should have experience with the
police system and its workings. This appreciation
of different styles is not for the purpose of
changing behavior, but rather for improving the
distinction of how police operate and how the
mental health services operate.

These are six general suggestions which may
serve to reduce the conflicts between the police
and mental health workers. They are not meant to
be all-inclusive. It is hoped that, by identifying
some of the trouble spots and providing these
strategies, both public services can continue to
do what they know how to do best.

REFERENCES

1. Bittner, Egon. Police Discretion in Emergency Apprehension of Mentally Ill Persons. *Social Problems* 1967, *14*, 278-292.

2. Liberman, R. Police as a community mental health resource. *Community Mental Health Journal*, 1969, *5*, 111-120.

3. Rokeach, M., Miller, M. G., and Snyder, J. A. The value gap between police and policed. *Journal of Social Issues*, 1971, *27*: 155-171.

4. Talbott, J. A. and Talbott, W. Training police in community relations and urban problems. *American Journal of Psychiatry*, 1971, *127* (7): 894-900.

5. Trojanowicz, C. The contrasting behavioral styles of policemen and social workers. *Public Personnel Review*, 1971, *32* (4): 246-251.

6. Whittington, H. G. The police: Ally or enemy of the comprehensive community mental health center? *Mental Hygiene*, 1971, *55*: 55-59.

SECTION III:

PROGRAM EXAMPLES:

CRISIS INTERVENTION AND COMMUNITY RELATIONS

5. CRISIS INTERVENTION: IMPLICATIONS FOR LAW ENFORCEMENT

Lieutenant Phillip York and Addison W. Somerville

In recent years there has been a running debate about the appropriate role for police in maintaining order in junior and senior high schools. While there are some who still advocate placing police in and around school buildings when there is a potential for disruption, many people with experience in this area (including police officers) believe that the presence of police often creates more problems than it resolves.

In Sacramento, California, the police department has adopted an approach which is different from those traditionally employed. They have placed police officers in school buildings -- but, not primarily for purposes of law enforcement. Instead, they function as counselors who attempt to prevent delinquency through establishing helping relations with youths who are experiencing personal problems.

This crisis intervention project, as described by Phil York, a police officer who was instrumental in initiating the program and Addison W. Sommerville, a psychology professor involved in training the counseling program, raises many questions for both the police and

67

*social scientists. For the police officer, it adds
another dimension   "counseling" to the list of
functions   which the officer must reconcile in
order to establish a viable role identity.   As
the amount of attention given to social problems
increases, the demands placed upon the law
enforcement officer seem to become greater.
For the social scientist, the use of police
officers in the role usually assumed by guidance
counselors, social workers, psychologists and
psychiatrists not only poses a direct threat
to their vested interests, but also creates
pressure on them to devise effective methods for
training these officers and evaluating the
impact   of their counseling on the youngsters
they counsel, on the schools and on the other
functions   performed by police in that community.*

      Today the court system is being utilized
as a referral agency to a greater extent than ever,
and children are being placed into the justice
system at an alarming rate.   Parental responsibilities are gradually being shifted to the police and
other social agencies.   However, too often the
difficulties are not with the child alone, but also
with the parents.   In these cases, misapprehensions
often can be dealt with more effectively if the
parent and youngster become directly involved in
the rehabilitative process, through participating
actively in a family counseling program.   When the
members gain insight into the causes of the problem
they often become more capable of coping with it.

      Furthermore, a person trained in crisis
counseling, who possesses an objective point of
view, can immediately intervene when it becomes
apparent that a breakdown in interpersonal relations
is occurring.

      As a part of a delinquency prevention
program project, the Youth Services Division of
the Sacramento Police Department has developed a
program to provide this type of intervention.

Efforts are directed toward the rehabilitation of
the minor who commits his *first* criminal offense.
Any youth who is referred to the Youth Services
Division and is not already on probation or parole
may be taken into the project. The parents are
contacted and arrangements are made for counseling
sessions at their earliest convenience with the
Youth Services Officer (YSD). Detention of the
youth is discouraged as this is a program designed
to test the feasibility of deferring the minors
out of the juvenile justice system.

Traditionally, delinquency prevention had
not been a primary function of law enforcement.
Although police often spoke of current prevention
measures being taken to decrease the incidence of
juvenile crime, closer examination revealed these
were really community relations projects. In
most cases, they had not dealt with the causes
of juvenile crime.

One exception was a very informal counseling
program initiated in 1960 by the Sacramento Police
Department. It involved abbreviated 15 minute
sessions with youths who had committed minor
offenses. The officers attempted to examine with
the youths the causes for their behavior. Although
they were untrained in psychological techniques,
a degree of success was accomplished; the recidivism
rate among those counseled was only 20 percent.
In view of this, it was speculated that a more
sophisticated and extensive counseling program might
prove to be a truly effective preventative measure.

As an integral part of this project, a
Youth Services Division Officer is assigned to each
of the eight high schools located in the City of
Sacramento. His objective as a member of the
Delinquency Prevention Project is to try to reduce
the present number of youthful offenders and to
bring about a decrease in the recidivism rate.

To attain these objectives, a concentrated

160 hour training program in crisis counseling
was designed and offered through Psychology
Department of California State University,
Sacramento. Twenty officers were trained in
appropriate and relevant skills for use in crisis
intervention with predelinquent youths and first
offenders. The training staff included persons
with skills in counselor training, school
psychology, clinical psychology, as well as a
statistician to objectively evaluate the project.
All of the staff members participated in tours
of duty with police officers prior to the
training program which helped make them more
knowledgeable about police field work.

The training involved 20 days of intensive
formal instruction. Each morning was devoted to
didactic classroom presentations. During the first
week the course orientation included an overview
of the area of delinquency, the dynamics of
delinquent behavior, the various concepts of
deviance, as well as the cultural factors which
must be considered when dealing with members of
various ethnic minority groups. The remainder
of the month concentrated upon the various counseling
theories and techniques which could be employed
by police officers. Special attention was given
to unique problems such as drug abuse, alcoholism,
suicide prone adolescents, family crises, and the
effects of parental (marital) problems upon youths.
Officers were trained in skills which would enable
them to deal with the youth in each situation
tactfully, causing a minimum of anxiety and
animosity.

Furthermore, in order for the officers to
acquire some counseling experience during the
training program it was decided to involve them
in followup interviews with youths who had been
issued juvenile citations for misdeameanor offenses.
Plans were made for three afternoons of counseling,
one week apart, at the Police Department. Each
officer taped his counseling session so that it

could be reviewed and evaluated by a staff member.

The afternoon sessions included field trips, movies, small group discussions, and training in the understanding of one's self and others. The officers presented a demanding, although refreshing, challenge to the training staff. In their eagerness to acquire the knowledge and expertise of a broad new field, they were impatient with anyone or anything that they did not immediately perceive to be totally relevant.

To alleviate this, each officer conferred individually with a staff member concerning any personal conflicts which may have arisen from the training. For the most part, the officers expressed fears of inadequacy during these conferences. They appeared to need reassurance and responded to the confidence shown in them. Several of the officers, responding to the climate of openness and acceptance, also discussed individual personal problems. Accepting the role of counselor may have enriched their understanding of the counseling relationship.

Working with the psychologists at California State University, Sacramento, was a new experience for the officers. Furthermore, in the past their contacts with school personnel had been limited to the routine reporting of juvenile offenders by the schools. School personnel had not been regarded as an important resource for dealing with the delinquent or predelinquent youth.

It must be pointed out that this has not been a program unmarred by problems. Many of these occurred simply because no guidelines were available. However, there were some that resulted from public suspicions of police becoming involved in a project which would identify and treat"predelinquents." Parents and students alike believed that the Youth Services Officer assigned to the school was there as an enforcer and an informer.

Although the school administrators approved of the placing of an officer in each of the high schools as crisis intervention counselors, it was members of the school counselor association, both local and statewide, who expressed concerns. They were afraid that the officers would attempt to deal with problems beyond their training and not restrict themselves to delinquent issues. After several meetings, however, roles were clarified and the issues were resolved. One of the primary causes for this misunderstanding was that the school persons did not feel that they had been included in the preliminary project planning. Their exclusion during the formulation stage was not intentional. In the designing of any future programs of this type, agencies which would be an integral part should be encouraged to participate in the planning.

Although the Youth Services Officer has occasion to interact with all school personnel, he works most closely with his field work consultant. A field work consultant is a counselor currently employed in a school setting, who is familiar with the operational procedures of the district as well as the intricacies of the staff, students, and community in which he is employed. He serves as a liaison and facilitator for the Youth Services Officer in his contacts with students, parents, school personnel, and the ongoing project consultants. This provides the Youth Services Officer with a resource for discussion and direction.

Young persons who seek out the Youth Services Officer for problems related to academic, family, or personal and social adjustments, are referred to a school counselor if their difficulties are not clearly related to delinquency. For example, a personality clash with a teacher warrants a sympathetic listener and a referral to another counselor for a possible shift of classes or some other appropriate action. However, if a girl is upset over a stormy relationship with her parents and is considering "running away," she may wish to discuss the general family situation. The Youth Services Officer should work with her to help prevent her contemplated delinquent action.

His role in the school is not one of a disciplinarian. He is a paraprofessional trained in the area of counseling, who possesses special skills related to law enforcement problems. He is more concerned with understanding and closely working with young people than in arresting them. It is hoped that through this approach fewer children and youths will ever have firsthand contact with detention and other hard core delinquents. Instead, it is believed that a positive interaction between our youth and law enforcement might help to decrease the mutual contempt, distrust, and animosity which has developed over the past decade.

The staff of police officers, who are assigned to the Delinquency Prevention Project, are selected from throughout the Police Department. Selection is not restricted to a job classification eligibility list. In this way candidates can be chosen on the basis of qualities that will benefit the community and the Department.

New officers who wish to participate in the program submit a written request to the unit commander. Selection is based on length of service, educational background, and desire to work with youth in the manner prescribed herein.

Officers are not assigned any criminal investigative work except that which involves child abuse, missing persons, and bicycle thefts. These are matters that seem germane to early delinquency patterns.

The Youth Services Officers review all juvenile arrests made by members of the Police

Department. They have the final determination
of whether to detain or release the youth after
consultation with the arresting officer, the
minor, and his/her parents. The specialized
crisis counseling training, which the Youth
Services Officer receives, permits him to
objectively make this decision. To assist him
in making these determinations, consultation
involving discussions of current cases are held
regularly with psychologists involved in the
program.

Every effort is made to bring the family
to a point where they may recognize and become
more capable of dealing with their problem as a
unit. In those cases in which long term counseling
is necessary, a suitable community service agency
is contacted and arrangements are made for
further counseling assistance.

The procedure for those to be counseled
is as follows: Individuals who have been cited
are scheduled for a Saturday counseling session
and the parents or guardian are notified by form
letter of the time and date that they are to
appear with the youth. In cases where the juvenile
is in custody, he is immediately assigned to the
counseling program. The counseling program is
explained to the adolescent and the parents, and
they are asked if they wish to participate.
Counseling is never undertaken unless there is
an attitude of cooperation on the part of the
parents as well as the delinquent.

The general response to this alternative
to incarceration or probation has been overwhelmingly
favorable. In no case has the family asked to
discontinue counseling or failed to maintain an
active interest. The parents, as well as the
adolescents, seem particularly pleased and impressed
when the YSD Officers show empathy and understanding
of their problems. Usually the officers make a
home visit or a phone call periodically to see

how the members of the family are progressing.
This often surprises and greatly pleases them.
The continued concern seems to give them support
and tends to further strengthen the positive
relationship previously established in the
counseling situation.

The most significant aspect of this
project is that it involves a completely new
approach toward handling juvenile delinquents.
Furthermore, it is a preventive program which
draws upon the experience and skills already
possessed by officers while at the same time
training them to fill a dual role of officer
and counselor.

Most other sophisticated programs in the
area of delinquency prevention are based upon
theoretical models and assumptions regarding the
causes of delinquency. The sociologically oriented
projects try to prevent and correct delinquency
by changing social conditions; among these are
approaches that utilize youth employment programs,
boys' clubs, recreation, urban planning and
community integration. Other programs are
psychologically oriented and attack the problem
by enhancing the ability of the individual to
cope and adjust.

It is unfortunate that most programs have
ignored the impact of the Youth Services Officer
and his influence in reducting the rate of
delinquency. ·This is not to say that a well
trained officer can be substituted for programs
to attack basic causes of delinquency, but the
idea cannot be ignored. Very few programs have
investigated the effect of psychological training
on the work of youth officers. It is easy to
brush the idea aside on the assumption that it
is difficult to make counselors out of police
personnel. It is regrettable, however, that with
proper techniques available, very few projects
have been willing to study the effect of the

police as an environmental and psychological variable.

This program has been based upon the assumption that the police officer is in an excellent position to be aware of the delinquent, as well as the pre-delinquent youth. He is in the most advantageous position to see family disturbances, the child who is being neglected, the juvenile gangs, and the potential "hot spots" of a neighborhood. He should therefore be considered one of the best persons in the community to intervene in a crisis situation.

The preliminary results of the project suggest that the techniques employed in this alternate method of dealing with first offenders might be utilized by other law enfocement agencies throughout the country. Between August 1, 1971 and March 31, 1974, the total number of juveniles arrested or cited for felony and misdemeanor offenses by the Sacramento Police Department was 11,998. Of these 3,856 minors, an equivalent of 32.1 percent were admitted into the Youth Services Division program. The total recidivism rate for these minors is 9.4 percent, a sharp contrast to the previous 20 percent.

It can be concluded, therefore, that persons possessing the skills and techniques of crisis counseling can detect the preliminary anxieties which accompany stress and by prompt intervention can help a family deal with the problem at the onset before it has developed into a highly complicated situation. By utilizing these counseling skills, some explosive situations which previously resulted in court referral can be avoided.

6. NOTHING BUT THE FACTS -- AND SOME
OBSERVATIONS OF NORMS AND VALUES:
THE HISTORY OF A CONSULTATION WITH
A METROPOLITAN POLICE DIVISION[1]

W. Brendon Reddy and Leonard M. Lansky[2]

*Among those approaches considered by
social science practitioners who wish to become
involved with police agencies, perhaps the most
popular is the human relations workshop. Many
practitioners believe that their greatest asset
and the police officers' greatest deficiency is
in the area of human relations skills.*

*W.Brendon Reddy and Leonard W. Lansky have
moved beyond the stage of contemplation and have
conducted a human relations training program with
officers of a large metropolitan police division.
Their paper not only presents the details of
their experience, but also contains an honest
appraisal of their attempts at influencing police
attitudes and behavior, and an analysis of the
critical value and norm conflicts which existed
between themselves, as change agents, and the
police officials they encountered.*

*The experiences and reflections which
Reddy and Lansky report might be helpful to those
who are giving serious consideration to developing
training programs involving social scientists
and police officers. Their paper underscores*

77

*the importance of dealing with the assumptions
and expectations of all parties involved in the
program, as well as attending to goals and
outcomes intended by those who initiate the
program.*

How do you see our police force? The
answer depends on who you are. It may also depend
upon your recent experiences. In urban centers,
if you are black or Appalachian and from the
inner city, black in a black suburb or long haired
and living in one of the "commune areas," you
are likely to have one set of attitudes and feelings
and experiences to go with them. If you are white,
living in a segregated area, you are likely to
have a different set of attitudes, feelings,
and experiences. If you work with a community
agency which mediates between the citizenry and
the police, you might have some unique feelings
and attitudes as well as some you share with
other groups.

"Knowing where one is" with regard to the
police is most important to the community change
agent. He must be able to look at his feelings
toward the police. Blindness to his own agenda,
values, and assumptions always limit the effectiveness of the helper. The issue is critical in
working with police.

The above is quite self-evident. Indeed it
was obvious to us, intellectually, as we began to
work with a metropolitan police division. But we
did not foresee our own blindness and the differences in values as we developed a relationship with
the police and other community agencies to initiate
an experiential human relations segment for the
police recruit training program. After briefly
reviewing the literature on norms and values of
police and community change agents, we present
the history of our work with the police.

VALUES AND NORMS

The attitudes and values of police have been well documented. The research confirms the stereotypes. On the average, police value loyalty and complete acceptance of orders (Preiss and Ehrlich, 1966); have a conservative political orientation (Guthrie, 1963); emphasize self control, obedience, and the comfortable life; generally they deemphasize freedom, equality, independence, the world of beauty, individual spontaneity, lenience, and tolerance (Rokeach, Miller, and Snyder, 1971); practice and advocate cohesion, solidarity, and secrecy within the force; employ traditional authoritarian, training procedures focusing on regulations rather than interpersonal skills, and tend to reject the core ideas and methods of sensitivity training (Skousen, 1967). The title of Skousen's paper sums up the value position: "Chief, watch out for those T-group promoters!" He advises that sensitivity training is designed to manipulate, alter, and destroy attitudes. Moreover, it is seen as anti-American and a discredit to the Judaic-Christian value system, a view shared by those with conservative political orientation.

These positions seem to be reinforced by selection procedures and occupational socialization (Rokeach et al., 1971). The constellation also approximates good psychological sense - survival sense, if you will - given the nature of the policeman's job and how it is seen by society. We are not apologizing for the attitudes, but the job is hazardous and underpaid. Police are usually called upon to react in immediate situations. While there is talk of long-run effectiveness, short-run is emphasized. For example, while the police divisions are quick to request workshops or training in principles of management, few divisions are willing to consider long term consultation.

Could one find a group with more contrasting values than change agents who focus on sensitivity training or variants thereof? This group of change agents values expanded consciousness and choice, a questioning scientific attitude, authenticity in interpersonal relations; openness in expressing feelings and ideas, collaboration with peers, underlings and authorities. They place emphasis on human concerns as well as the task, the *processes* of working as well as the content of work, on-going diagnosis and reexamination rather than dogmatically held rules and principles, a questioning of authority, of rules and regulations, a tolerance for ambiguity in learning and human relationships,an openness to intra- and interpersonal conflict and new ways for resolving the same, relatively liberal political and social values, and, lastly, a learning model which emphasizes process as well as content, and the affective as well as the cognitive.

PRECIPITATING INCIDENT AND EARLY HISTORY--ENTRY

The initial incident was a claim of police brutality. A pregnant woman, the wife of a white Presbyterian minister, was arrested during a civil demonstration and taken to a police detention area. Her husband brought the incident to the attention of the City Religious Coalition (CRC) which, in its three years of existence, had begun to gain credibility and visibility with its member churches (almost all of the denominations in the city) and city leaders. The driving force behind the coalition was its executive director, a young minister with a quiet but strong manner and a commitment to change in the community. During this same period, the Municipal Human Relations Commission (MHRC), an independently contracted representative of municipal government, had completed a survey of city employment of minorities, especially blacks. MHRC and CRC had been discussing ways to encourage the city to recruit and promote minorities, especially in the fire and police

departments. Thus, the executive director of
CRC naturally asked MHRC to join him in approach-
ing the Police Division about the incident.

There was considerable informal contact
among the executive director, the police
specialists in MHRC, the safety director of the
city, various councilmen, and the top leadership
of the Police Division. There was at least one
meeting between the safety director of the city
and CRC's executive committee. Following that
meeting which occurred two months after the
incident, informal meetings continued. It was
reported that the safety director had instructed
the Police Division"to take the matter seriously."
CRC and MHRC focused on the need for change,
preferably some training. At one time, the CRC
recommended a training program for sergeants and
those in higher ranks. That idea was turned down
It was not until four months after the incident
that final agreement was reached among CRC. MHRC
and the Police Division to add two weeks to *the*
training of the next recruit class, to be paid
for by CRC. CRC was to arrange the program with
the Police Division because: (1) CRC was not a
direct arm of the city; (2) CRC was funding it.

Two weeks later, CRC asked an Episcopal
Church trainer to assist them. She suggested the
Community Psychology Institute talk with CRC.
The Community Psychology Institute(CPI) is a
nonprofit community consultation and service
arm of the University of Cincinnati, Department
of Psychology. It functions as a training and
research agency concerned with the development
of consultation skills in advanced doctoral
students in clinical and social psychology.
Our notion of community psychology is based upon
the organizational development and change
emphasis in applied behavioural science.

So far as we know, the executive director's
call to us was the first contact by CRC or the

Police Division with any consultants in human
relations or organizational development.   However,
as we shall see, there was an ongoing program in
"sensitivity training" for the Police Division
being conducted bv another group of consultants.

The authors, as representatives of the
Community Psychology Institute, met with the
executive director of CRC. He reviewed the
history and shared his perceptions about the
Police Division, especially points of resistance
and power. His directive, as mediator between
the Police Division, the angry faction of community, and any potential training staff, was to
arrange a meeting with the second in command
(sergeant) of the Police Division's Training
Section. The agenda was "to explore" the proposed
human relations training program for recruits,
even though the sergeant admitted that the
Division saw any such program as an imposition
on the Training Section. We accepted his statements as diagnostic data, indicated our doubts
about working only with recruits, but continued
to explore possible dates, facilities, and handling
of budgets. We also described our experiential
approach to human relations training, at its
mildest a radical program for any traditional,
conservative law enforcement agency. The sergeant
indicated that the Division already had an interpersonal relations program which did not upset
anyone in the Division.

Although we had requested it, at this time
we did not have direct contact with the top of
the organization or of the Training Section. A
few days after the initial meeting, the first
author was called by a higher ranking officer
from the Training Section who was quite annoyed
that the new program seemed to be "out of the
hands of the Police Division." He reemphasized
pointedly, "it is our program for our recruits."
He requested a meeting for all parties concerned.

A few days later, the authors, a police lieutenant colonel, his captain in charge of the Training Section, a sergeant, and a member of MHRC (the only black person present) met. Since this meeting was to be on operations, the executive director of CRC did not attend. Our agenda included: (1) opening up communication among the attending, interested, and contributing groups to the human relations training; (2) clarifying the various roles regarding MHRC, CRC, the Police Division, CPI, and any pressure groups; (3) checking each group's expectations about the training programs, goals, and measures of success; (4) determining the training staff; (5) any other agenda items. Two facts were accepted, albeit reluctantly by all: (1) there was to be some human relations training; (2) it would be for recruits only. The police were openly resistant to the first. They felt that they already had human relations training. They did a series of lectures on the topic. Furthermore, they felt that this program was being forced on them. The MHRC and CPI representatives were unhappy with the decision to work only with recruits. It was obvious that recruits were the least likely group to influence what was happening in the Division or on the street.

Because of these feelings and history, the meeting was stressful. Identifying goals was difficult. The police officials strongly disagreed with the CPI staff which suggested a cross-cultural, experiential program conducted by a team of black and white trainers. The police training staff advocated a structured lecture-type program on black history, the psychology of rumor, and "techniques" on how to deal with minorities. The police knew that CRC and MHRC supported the CPI proposal. The training captain repeatedly stressed that he wanted considerable structure and wished to avoid open conflict. The CPI staff countered that the objective was to learn to deal constructively with conflict. After considerable

discussion, the lieutenant colonel seemed
satisfied with the general statement of goals,
namely, that the recruit class learn to be more
effective in their interpersonal relations with
white and black policemen, supervisors, and
community people.

Another point of strain was the police
staff's wish that we provide in advance an hour-
by-hour outline of the program. It was difficult
for them to accept our strategy of diagnosing,
planning, and designing in response to the
reactions of the recruits.

During the meeting the MHRC official was
rather quiet. Afterwards, he was quite vocal
about what he felt were the racist attitudes of
the police. He wanted the recruits to have
direct contact with blacks, Appalachians, "hippies",
and poor people in various neighborhoods.

The critical issue of assessing the program
were left vague. CPI and police each agreed to
evaluate separately.

A few weeks later, the authors visited a
session on human relations at the police training
academy. The setting was formal, with recruits
sitting in straight even rows. The lecturer, an
officer on the force, presented some basic
psychology. There was no dialogue or discussion.

Two days before the workshop, a lieutenant
colonel in charge of the Police Community Relations
Bureau called the first author to insist that an
"objective observer" be present during all workshop sessions in order that "a good evaluation
be done." Although the lieutenant colonel had
not been involved in the early negotiations nor
was he in the training section, he was interested
in terms of his own bureau's community programs.
The first author explained that while we welcomed
an evaluation and would be doing our own, we

were concerned that nonparticipating observers
would introduce an entirely different set of
variables which might preclude our conducting
an effective workshop. While he remained
verbally adamant, the lietenant colonel did not
send his "observer."

The planning took place at CPI the day
before the workshop. The all-day session was
disrupted by several phone calls from the captain
of the Training Division who indicated that he
could not spare anyone to participate fully in
the workshop. He wanted his staff "to supervise"
by walking in occasionally "to check up on things."
He would not hear any discussion to the contrary,
insisting that he must be responsible for "*his*
men and *his* program." The first author accepted
his concerns and sense of responsibility but also
reemphasized the potential harm of this procedure.
After a lengthy discussion the author felt that
some understanding had been effected for the CPI
point of view. He them summarized the conversation.
The captain indicated he would see the staff the
following day.

Observations of the Entry Phase

While the advocating agencies such as CRC
and MHRC were painfully aware that "something"
should be done, they seemed to be unaware of many
alternatives. Although they felt that traditional
teaching was not the answer, their only alternative
was a "two week sensitivity session." Like the
police, they did not use outside consultants early
in their planning. The police, however, because
of their norms and values maintained that teacher/
student, supervisor/recruit was the preferred,
if not the only, way to go. Unfortunately this
view was strengthened by the consultants that had
been conducting the "sensitivity training,"
mentioned above, with all levels of the Police
Division.

In groups of 20-30, officers had participated
in a three-day residential program consisting of
lectures and role-playing exercises labelled
"sensitivity training." The program did not
include any T-group experience or strong confrontations about problems of race or other prejudices.
Yet, these programs were sensitizing police officers
to the importance of talking more openly about
human relations' issues. Indeed, as of this
writing, mainly through its own efforts with help
from MHRC, the program is more confronting and
provides practice in dealing with strongly held
prejudicial feelings, attitudes, and behaviors.
However, at the time of the incidents described
here, the Police Division's image was that
human relations training consisted of non-threat-
ening presentations. Yet the leaders of the
"sensitivity"program had not been approached by
the Police Division or CRC in this instance.

The failure to use known resources is
puzzling. There was pressure from CRC and MHRC;
the police are used to making quick decisions.
Why did they not turn at once to their resources?
One hunch is not very complimentary to our
colleagues or ourselves although it fits our
experience. At that time, the Division had little
investment in human relations. The ongoing
program was accepted just because it neither
threatened nor opened up conflict. By not threatening the system, our counterparts may have
achieved sufficient trust to then move to other
levels in their training programs. At the time
the recruit program was planned, however, they
were not seen as resources by the Police Division,
CRC, or MHRC.

Such relatively poor use of resources, the
focusing on the narrow issue, and looking for some
"expert" or "vendor" to provide a short term
solution - these strategies seem endemic to many
public organizations: police divisions, schools,
city governments. The long-term organizational

development approach is still virtually unknown
in such systems. Unfortunately, there are many
"experts" willing to try to work on some fraction
of the underlying problem. We did so. A major
social issue is educating such systems to think
more in terms of long range planning for their
missions, their structure, and their personnel.

The police could not accept the conditions
of an organizational development approach. The
logic of working first with "top" administrators
did not make sense to them- or it made too much
sense and was too threatening. As the situation
has been in many organizations - schools, industry,
social agencies- entry was made at lower levels.
Although CRC suggested that training start at
least at a sergeants' level, the Division, we do
not know who or under what circumstances, insisted
that we begin with recruits. Thus, the only
alternative fit the demands of the police. That
decision presented a professional and theoretical
dilemma to the CPI staff: should we enter the
system at all if it could only be at the level
of recruits? And only with lower level contact?
For a number of reasons we agreed although we
were fully aware that we might fail to have much
influence on the recruits or the Division. We
wanted to respond to the needs and interests of
the community; and if we were successful in
introducing some new concepts of learning,
problem-solving, acknowledging and understanding
racism, we might then have the visibility and
trust to explore other collaborative programs
and/or consultations. There were some negative
results. Since the highest levels of police
administration were minimally involved in the
process and did not participate in the program,
there was little motivation and commitment to
it. Indeed, there was, as might be expected,
anger, mistrust, and suspicion regarding CPI's
motives and design.

We, the CPI staff, also erred in not

including black colleagues at the onset of
negotiations. Given the racial tensions in our
society collaborative work by black and white
professionals can have many positive effects.
The perceptions, modeling, sensitivity, and
cultural insights of black staff and black/
white collaboration as staff are essential in
any biracial community program, permitting
racial issues to emerge and be dealt with in
ways which are not possible in all white
professional or lay groups.

There were other things we might have
done. While we did visit one class, we did
not accept an invitation to visit the class
while it was on the firing range. Nor did we
explore the possibility of our riding with
regular patrolmen in order to learn more about
the Division. Thus, the charge that "you
really do not know about police" had considerable
validity. We might have anticipated the difficulty
to be reported below concerning the presence of
someone from the Division during the program.
The first hint occurred when we did not work
through the issue of evaluation; the second came
with the several phone calls during the planning
session. We assumed all would turn out fine.

We have many speculations about the causes
of these actions and inactions. Certainly we
were eager to establish a working relationship
with the Police Division. Thus, we might have
hesitated to push on controversial issues such
as evaluation. We also held rather negative
stereotypes about police officers and police
organizations. These attitudes help account for
our failure to take the obvious steps of learning
more about the police by informal contacts and
extensive visits on their turf. While we worked
through many of these issues during the program,
we also learned again how important it is to
work continuously at getting our own "heads in
order" while working with any group.

The Recruit Program

A detailed account of the first 80 hours
(and its evaluation) is available from the first
author. This section contains the barest outline.

Rationale

CRC's proposal, accepted by police and
CPI, included time for police and community groups
to meet each other in a controlled setting to
exchange information, and to express feelings.
Thus, the staff developed a cross-cultural,
experiential training design. The major
differences between it and the traditional classroom model have been described by Harrison and
Hopkins (1967, pp.437-438):[3]

Traditional Classroom	*Cross-Cultural Training*
Source of Information	
Information comes from experts through the media of books, lectures, and audio-visual presentations.	Information sources must be developed by the learner from the social environment. Methods include observation and questioning of associates and other learners.
Learning Settings	
Learning takes place in settings such as class-rooms, libraries, etc.	The entire social environment is the setting for learning. Every human encounter provides relevant information.
Problem-Solving Approaches	
Problems are defined and posed to the learner by experts and	The learner is on his own to define problems, generate hypotheses,

authorities. Methods are specified, and the student's work is checked for accuracy. The emphasis is on solutions to known problems.

and collect data from the social environment. The emphasis is on discovering problem-solving approaches on the spot.

Traditional Class room   *Cross-Cultural Training*

Role of Emotions and Values

Problems are largely dealt with at an ideational level. Questions of reason and of fact are paramount. Feelings and values may be discussed, but are rarely acted upon.

Problems are usually value-and emotion laden. Facts are often less relevant than the perceptions and attitudes which people hold. Values and feelings have action consequences, and action must be taken.

Criteria of Successful Learning

Favorable evaluation by experts and authorities of the quality of the individual's productions, primarily written work.

The establishment and maintenance of effective and satisfying relationships with others in the work setting. This includes the ability to communicate with and influence others.

The Staff

The staff were selected on the bases of race, sex, training experience, locality, availability and interest, and participant ratio. We wished to work in male/female biracial teams with 12 to 15 participants. At the time of the program, however, there were few female trainers, black or white, in the metropolitan area who were interested or available. The workshop staff were five males, two whites, three black, and one white

woman. All but one staff person were from the
metropolitan area and all were familiar with the
Police Division. Only one, however, the first
author, had previously worked with police
personnel.

Participants

There were 39 police participants; 32 men
(31 white and 1 black) and 1 woman were affliated
with the Metropolitan Police Division; 5 men were
from nearby suburban departments; of the
Metropolitan recruits, 18 were in a two year
university cadet program. The 39th participant
was a training sergeant who took part as a
regular group member.

As part of their training, the cadets had
ridden on regular shifts with veteran police
officers. They had also served in other capaci-
ties in various offices throughout the Division.

One day of the program included 15 college
age youths from a local university, VISTA, and
the inner city; a second day involved 15 black
residents of the inner city.

Overview

Because of time pressure and constraints
in the entire police training program, the
community relations portion was spread over a
four week period. The first 40 hours focused on
personal skills in communication, the multiplicity
of roles of the participants, the legitimacy of
feelings, problem-solving and decision-making
behaviors, and dealing with critical and
potentially escalating community situations. The
goals were to permit participants to examine their
behaviors and feelings in a supportive atmoshphere
Another goal was to develop mutual support among
the recruits. The cross-cultural design and
biracial staff permitted the planned introduction

of racial issues. Each day ended with a
community meeting of participants and staff to
share learnings and feelings. These sessions
provided diagnostic information for planning
the following day's design.

The design began with a series of
communication exercises, moved into issues of
interpersonal feedback and racial awareness and
attitudes, and then focused on team - building
exercises using problem-solving and decision-
making activities. In the final phase, all the
previous work was brought to bear on the meetings
with people from the community. The small group
format, called "D" for "discussion" group, was
used regularly to examine the learnings from the
more structured activities.

The Workshop Experience

The workshop opened on rather shaky
grounds. The recruits were in the final weeks of
their 22 week long program. They had been told
some important facts: they knew that someone
from the university was going to do a "sensitivity
training" program with them and that it was
initiated by the community and not by the Police
Division. Moreover, as we found out later, some
veteran officers had told the cadets that the
whole idea would undoubtedly be a waste of time;
some superiors had commented that the program
was not theirs but only a response to pressure
from the public. Since the 80 hours of human
relations training were added to the recruit
training after the class had begun, it meant
that recruits would now have to postpone gradu-
ation for two weeks. All these factors
generated rather intense hostility and resistance.

The first author opened the workshop with
the usual remarks about human relations training
and commented on the publicity given to the
police human relations training program. He

also outlined some major events, including the
plans to meet with two different groups of
citizens. The recruits, sitting in very
straight even rows, barely responded. When the
author told the recruits that anyone coming into
the program would be asked to participate, the
captain in charge of training, standing in the
rear of the room, turned to the second author
and quietly commented, "That's not the way it's
going to be." The second author alerted his
colleague about the comment. During the first
exercise, and away from the participants, the
authors had an intense confrontation with the
captain on the issue which supposedly had been
settled on the telephone the day before. The
captain insisted it was our understanding and
not his that supervisors would participate fully.
At this point the second author felt strongly
that we were being co-opted and indicated we
would terminate the program at that point if we
could not follow the agreed upon ground rules.
The ranking officer left the discussion and
contacted the acting chief, the safety director,
and the Division lieutenant colonel. They
decided, without further consulting the CPI
staff, that a sergeant on the training staff
would spend the entire time participating in the
program. The captain did not appear again in
the actual program; the sergeant participated
throughout.

        From the first day, recruits were suspicious
and restive, they did not want to talk about race.
Resistance on social matters was not the only
problem. The recruits were accustomed to a very
traditional teaching-learning situation. Most
found it very difficult to see any relationships
between the "game" situations used in training
and the live settings they would be working in.
It was difficult for the staff to imagine at this
point that the program would turn out successfully.

        The situation changed. Several recruits

began to share their feelings; considerable "unfreezing" (Lewin, 1951; Schein and Bennis, 1965) occurred.   However, a few remained completely resistive and convinced that our responsibility was strictly to tell them what to do. Two events are instructive.

During the second 40 hours, several recruits complained that we were not presenting real-life situations that concerned them.   Thus, small groups were asked to design a role playing activity to dramatize a situation which might escalate.   After putting on their "skits",the entire group would discuss them.

Each group picked a difficult situation, e.g., a sit-in by "hippies," a fight in a bar. Furthermore, each role playing situation ended in violence.   While some recruits discussed alternative approaches to each situation, many insisted that the staff had "set up" the role playing situations to prove (self-fulfill) that "all cops are violent."   Many recruits could not take responsibility for their own behavior.

The second event occurred on the next to the last day of the program.   We were invited to a neighborhood house in a downtown black community to meet with some young adults to "rap" about "police-community relations."   Prior to the formal program, several recruits who attempted to make contact with the Blacks were rejected; the residents would not speak to them.   During the program, the community's representatives forcefully presented their views of the police. The effect was sobering.   Again, however, several recruits found it almost impossible to hear the messages.   They said that the staff and community were out to get them.   Others responded differently.   They shared, under considerable strain, that they had begun to hear in a new way how the Blacks felt towards the police.   The last day was a difficult one, not only because of the

previous experience. The recruits received
their uniform jackets, belts, and guns. They
had one week to go before the end of training.

Observations on the Workshop

"Don't rock the boat."
"The outside is against us - noone understands us."
"Feelings are irrelevant on the job; they
are also irrelevant in education - just tell us
the facts."
These sentiments were evident in the first
days of the program.

The first encounter with the ranking officer
was an attempt to keep things under control. By
"dropping in" whenever he wished, he could insure
that the recruits would not feel free to share
openly. By restricting the program to recruits
or including some administrators as full participants, we hoped to lessen the recruits' resistance.
We were only partially successful. The training
officer (sergeant) in the program focused on the
importance of self-control and police procedures,
whatever the topic being discussed, while our goal
was to have the recruits (and the sergeant) become
more aware of the forces to be controlled and the
choices of methods. We were, for a considerable
time, working at cross purposes. Indeed, it was
not until the last day that the sergeant shared
strong personal feelings about some earlier
experiences while empathizing with a recruit who
expressed anxiety about having to use violence.
That sharing opened a flood of feelings from the
group; the shift in level of relating - listening,
acceptance, sharing - was palpable. At that
point, the sergeant began to act differently
towards the staff and our methods. He then
accepted our approach and openly expressed trust
in our skills.

Throughout, the recruits and the sergeant

were in a dilemma. They were in the training
program and we were the "instructors." They felt
an obligation to participate. They knew there
would be no tests and no reports on who did what.
Yet they had been told by veteran officers and
superiors that we were forced on them by the
community. How were they to resolve - these were
recruits - the conflict between duty to the
community and pressure from their peers and
superiors. The inner conflict was considerable.
Some were very much part of the "now" generation.
Prior to joining the force, they too had long
hair. Several had had some "contacts" with police
as teenagers; others had tried pot. Their
preferred music was rock; they were divided in
views about Vietnam. To several, much of our
philosophy and approach made sense. However,
others were sons or nephews of policemen and
firemen. They got strong opposition to the ideas
in the program upon returning home every evening
and on weekends. All these data pointed up the
importance of a program that goes far beyond the
recruit class.

The CPI staff had both overestimated and
underestimated the recruits. We had underestimated
the resistance in the system and, alas, we were
quite blind to the depth of our own stereotypes
and prejudices against the police. The biases got
in our way. However, we shared our own learnings
with the recruits and spent considerable time in
our staff meetings on these issues. We do not
know, of course, to what extent our attitudes
affected the design. For example, would we have
designed the visit to the neighborhood houses
earlier if we had been more in touch with our
own enmities towards the police? Would that have
helped?

The recruits were an articulate, intelligent
group of young men. We had not expected them to
be verbal; we had not expected the wide range of
interests we discovered. We also underestimated

their resistance to change. We arrived during
the last four weeks of their training cycle.
Thus, we could not judge how much resistance
represented: their socialization into their role
as police officers; their resentment at having to
delay getting to the field, and their anxiety
about it; or more enduring personality tendencies.
We also underestimated the additional difficulty
for us and the recruits in having a training
officer present throughout the program. In the
long run, his presence turned out to be an asset.
As he began to learn from our program, he served
as a model, in-house, which recruits could more
readily follow. His responses on the last day
had an imprtant impact on the recruits and on
further negotiations with the Training Division.

Evaluation and Hindsight

It should be no surprise that we feel that
the program was successful and unsuccessful in
both short- and long-range objectives. Nor should
it surprise anyone that we have very little hard
data to back up our appraisals. We are still a
long way from working with social change programs
that permit effective research designs. Furthermore, as amply discussed in the literature, there
is a serious question about how to go at such
research (Campbell and Stanley, 1963; Argyris, 1970;
Weiss and Rein, 1972; Weiss, 1972).

The most solid information is on the recruits'
immediate reactions to the program. They filled
out an evaluation questionnaire at the closing
session to help us in planning future programs.
A complete report is available from the first
author. The results were encouraging. Three-
quarters of the recruits showed considerable
change and awareness of racial issues. A few
maintained both mistrust of the staff, the process,
and their previous feelings and attitudes about
police work, blacks, the poor, and the like.
This few, and others, reported negative feelings

about what they saw as the community's forcing
the program on them; several resented our keeping
them in classes an additional two weeks that they
could be out learning and doing their jobs.

We have already commented on the pressure
towards these feelings from experienced officers,
the training sergeant, and some other superiors.
Our training model itself caused difficulty,
even among those recruits who had experienced
similar classes in their cadet training. We
believe other forces, structural ones, also
contributed to the resistance and to lessening
its impact: (1) its lateness in the total recruit
program; (2) fragmentation of the 80 hours; (3)
its nonresidential nature. We recommended changes
in all three for future programs. We also recommended follow-up for the recruits themselves and
parallel programs for superior and veteran officers.
Our view, substantiated by work from other
interventions (Schmuck and Miles, 1971; Argyris,
1970), is that the values and behaviors must be
reinforced and supported in order to change the
behaviors of the police and the Division.

Here we have some encouraging and
discouraging data about long range effects. A
first encouragement came in the Division's agreeing to a program for the next recruit class.
However, because of confusions with the city
council about budgeting, the program did not
occur. The protests about the omission from
members of council, CRC, MHRC, and others lead
to the planning and execution of a program for
the very next class - i.e., one entire recruit
class, about 40 men and women, was skipped. The
Police Division also agreed to two of the three
structural changes - having 40 hours of the
program early in the class's history and 40 later
on. They did not agree, however, to a residential
program even though there is precedent for such
a program in the residential programs described
earlier.

Our second effort at human relations
training in the Police Division will be described
elsewhere. Suffice it to say, we confirmed our
previous notions about police norms and values,
especially the urgency of direct work with
experienced and superior officers. The Police
Training Division agreed with us; our second
report stated unequivocally that we would not
entertain future programs with recruits unless
there were parallel efforts at other levels.
The immediate data on the program itself
surprised us in part. The first phase of the
program, held the second week in the recruits'
training, was seen as very helpful and effective
by more than three-fourths of the men. The
second phase of the program, however, held the
second to the last week of their training, was
rejected by more than 50%. During the interval
between the two sessions we conducted, the
recruit class had several lectures and other
exposures to human relations and race relations.
One response was that they were "fed up" with
the material; another response reflected the
previous classes' view. That is, all this
"stuff" was quite irrelevant and being forced
on them. They perceived it would be very
different when they got on the street.

The outcome of the second program was
clearcut. No further work has even been discussed.
This outcome is surprising because later recruit
classes had as many as 50% blacks whereas previously there were only one or two out of the total of
40-50 recruits. The meaning of this action is
not completely clear, however. Before explaining
our caution, we have to put the events in context.

Our efforts did not occur in a vacuum.
There has been much concern with "law and order,"
crime, and racial tensions in our society. As
our first program was being planned, new funds
(LEAA) were being provided for assisting police
divisions with their organizational structures,

equipment, and training of patrolmen. The present city was in the forefront of several such efforts. One grant focused on a community sector program, which put teams of patrolmen back on the beat in several sectors of the inner city with histories of high crime rates and poor police - community relationships. Another large scale program aims at the Division's community and human relations program through direct contact with the public and increased hiring of minority group members. The expanded cadet program includes police training and a two year university associate's degree. Because of increasing number of projects and resources and the involvement of the municipal university,a police/university consortium has been formed.

Ongoing training has been built into the Division for many years. A subcommittee of the consortium is currently planning a human relations segment which will become part of the sequence provided for sergeants on the force. On the other hand, so far as we know, the community sector training program did not include any consultation from human relations' consultants.

Did we make the right decision in accepting the original contract? On balance do we thing our inputs have been positive or negative? We do not know. We think we helped some men and women see the potential in some different norms in police work. We also think we had some impact on the system. Our reports have been circulated widely within the force, the staff and board of CRC, MHRC, and the city council. Yet, we must accept that the basic norms and values of the Police Division do not seem to have changed very much. In speaking about the new community sector program, the local paper reported that the "City Safety Director...is not even hinting that the program will fail. But if it should not be extended, the experience and knowledge gained will make it all worthwhile, he says." Need we spell out the double message or potential self-fulfilling prophecy?[4]

Can we be more definite? Yes. We would - with high probability - do the same thing again, that is, take on the contract with all its limitations, even at the Police Training Academy and with limited time. We agree with Harrison (1970) that one does well to take a client where he is at.....at least at first. However, as we became clearer about the total situation and the strength of the norms, we again would probably have repeated our refusal to go on without more concessions from the system. To date we have not been asked to do any specific work. However, we must note that our test is weak. The intervening months, the concern and action about law and order, the development of other programs by the police including the continuance and strengthening of the residential "sensitivity" program described above -- all these make it impossible to test our effects directly.

REFERENCES

1. Argyris, C. *Invervention theory and method: A behavioral science view.* Reading, Massachusetts: Addison-Wesley, 1970.

2. Campbell, D.T. and Stanley, J.C *Experimental and quasi-experimental designs for research on teaching.* In N.L. Gage (Ed.) *Handbook of Research on Teaching.* Chicago: Rand McNally, 1963.

3. Guthrie, C.R. Law enforcement and the juvenile: A study of police interaction with delinquents. Unpublished doctoral dissertation, School of Public Administration, University of Southern California, 1963.

4. Harrison, R. Choosing the depth of organizational intervention. *Journal of Applied Behavioral Science,* 1970, 6, 181-202.

5. Harrison, R. and Hopkins, R.L. The design of cross-cultural training: An alternative to the university model. *Journal of Applied Behavioral Science,* 1967, 3, 431-460.

6. Lewin, K. *Field theory in social science.* New York: Harper, 1951.

7. Preiss, J.J. and Ehrlich, H.J. *An Examination of Role Theory: The case of the state police.* Lincoln, Nebraska: University of Nebraska Press, 1966.

102

8. Rokeach, M., Miller, M.G. and Snyder, J.A.
   The value gap between police and policed.
   Journal of Social Issues, 1971, 27, 155-171.

9. Schein, E. H. and Bennis, W.G. *Personal and
   Organizational Change through Group Methods.*
   New York: Wiley, 1965.

10. Schmuck, R.A. and Miles, M.B. (Eds.)
    Organizational Development in Schools.
    Palo Alto, California: National Press
    Books, 1971.

11. Skousen, W.C. Chief, watch out for those
    T-group promoters! *Law and Order,*1967,
    70, 10-12.

12. Weiss, C.H. *Evaluating action programs:
    Readings in social action and education.*
    Boston: Allyn and Bacon, 1972.

13. Weiss, R.S. and Rein, M. The evaluation of
    broad-aim programs: Experimental design,
    its difficulties, and an alternative.
    Administrative Science Quarterly, 1970,
    15, 97-109.

FOOTNOTES

[1]By permission of *The Journal of Social Issues,*
Vol. 30.

[2]The authors gratefully acknowledge the contributions
of their colleagues to the project: Betty Crosset,
Halloway C. Sells, Harvey Reed, Frank Williams.

[3]Quoted by permission of NTL Institute for Applied
Behavioral Science.

[4]This sentence was written in 1973. In the Fall of
1974, even in the face of inflation, the community-
sector program was expanded.

7. UNDERSTANDING AND ALLEVIATING CONDITIONS LEADING TO CONFRONTATION BETWEEN YOUTH AND AUTHORITY: RECOMMENDATIONS FOR A WORKING PROGRAM MODEL[1]

Robert Cohen and Sidney Oglesby

"What are we going to do about the other generation?" reads the line from the popular show tune from a few years back. "Generation gap" was another phrase we found ourselves using to label a whole series of problems involving younger and older members of society. But singing about it, or labeling it is never enough, even though we may feel that once we have labeled the situation we will then be able to deal with the problems arising from it. Indeed, interactions between youths and adults, particularly adults in positions of authority, have probably always been volatile and potential sources of conflict. They become issues of relevance to police and social scientists when the conflicts become disorders, and we say to ourselves that something ought to be done to avoid needless hurt, destruction, violence, criminalization.

Robert Cohen and Sidney Oglesby address themselves to the task of developing a preventive method for dealing with confrontations between youth and authority. They deal with the implementation of training programs which include such activities as discussions, role-playing, testing exercises, simulations, readings, and panels.

105

*The model which they propose includes three
major phases: The first focuses on improving
communication among the participants; the second
aims at developing an understanding of the
conditions and problems which lead to confrontation; and the third involves the development
and implementation of strategies for alleviating
the conditions, and resolving the problems which
produce confrontation.   The effect is to move
quickly from the abstract to the concrete - to
detail the steps one would go through in
developing a particular training program
intended to be responsive to the needs of
individuals involved in youth - authority interactions, and to emphasize the preventive aspects
of these endeavors.*

*As young people become more outspoken in
their demands for recognition as mature individuals,
those in positions of authority find themselves
needing to consider a greater range of behavorial
options in order to cope with their responsibilities.
If their responses are not effective, a confrontation
usually arises, which is typically accompanied
by side effects of frustration, turmoil and
disruption.   In most instances, law enforcement
officers, and other authority figures, are then
required to deal with the manifestations of
confrontation in order to "cool" the situation.
While this may reduce the immediate flare-up,
it usually does nothing to resolve the causes and
conditions which initailly produced the confrontation.
Consequently, there is a strong possiblity that
some form of confrontation will recur.*

*The logical progression from this argument
would be to develop methods for dealing with the
conditions which lead to confrontation before a
crisis erupts.   Following this preventive approach
not only offers the advantage of getting closer
to the source of the problem in a manner which
may lead to a long term resolution, but also
reduces the likelihood of violent confrontation.*

Having stated the merits of the preventive method, it is also necessary to point out some of the difficulties inherent in this approach. First, it requires planning and foresight, qualities which are in short supply in this era in which so much of our energy is consumed in merely trying to survive the seemingly endless series of crises that beset us. Second, the concept of prevention often appears to be vague, abstract and complex. It is an illusory concept, which makes theoretical sense, but is difficult to operationalize. Finally, a strong commitment is required from all participants in a preventive endeavor, and the interpersonal interaction involved in implementing a successful preventive program in the area of confrontation are intense and may easily degenerate unless properly facilitated.

This paper describes a working model for conducting programs directed at promoting understanding and working toward alleviating those conditions which lead to confrontation between youth and authority. The model was derived from a number of training programs involving young people and adults, but it comes particularly from a program conducted for a group of high school students, police officers, teachers, guidance counselors and other adults who work with youngsters. A brief description of the youth-authority confrontation program is provided before presenting the program model which has been developed.

The Youth-Authority Confrontation Project

The intended purpose of this project was to develop techniques for dealing with confrontations between youth and persons in positions of authority, as well as training a specific group of individuals to handle intergroup and interpersonal problems. The major phase of the Confrontation Project was a series of workshops

conducted by social science practitioners.
Financial support for the project was obtained
from the State Department of Education. Overall
administration of the project was the responsibility of the University's Continuing Education
Center. The actual implementation of the project
was conducted by members of the Institute for
Community Psychology at Syracuse University
(now Institute for Community Development). This
organization provided staff which conducted the
project and an evaluation staff which attempted
to measure progress toward the stated goals of
the project.

Stated Goals:

The stated objectives of the Confrontation
Project were :

1) Improve the understanding of specific
teachers, policemen, guidance counselors or social
workers regarding the bases or sources of conflict
situations involving youth.
2) Improve the understanding and skills
of these personnel regarding the resolution of
specific and realistic conflict situations.
3) Provide actual practice in applying
communications skills and the principles of
human relations to resolve interpersonal and
intergroup problems.
4) Extend the understanding and skills
developed in the program to other audiences
through the development of materials and methods
to be used in police and teacher inservice
training programs.

There are then two separate but inter-
dependent sets of goals for the project. The
training and experience of specific participants
can be looked at as the process of dealing with
the confrontation situation, while the resultant
techniques developed can be conceptualized as
the product of the project.

The Process:

The principle activity of the project was a five month workshop comprised of thirteen meetings between October, 1970 and February, 1971. In addition, consultations between staff members and participants took place during and subsequent to the workshop. Meetings took place on specified Sunday and Monday evenings, the former usually lasting seven hours, the latter for three hours.

Selection of Participants

Participants for this project were selected on the basis of expected relevance to the confrontation situation. These people were generally volunteers from among the following groups:

Students	(6)
Teachers	(4)
Police	(6)
Community People	(3)
Guidance Counselors	(3)

Care was taken to select a representative number of both black and white participants. Participants were compensated for their efforts with tuition remittance, stipends, and work time (police). Most of the participants selected from the school system were affiliated with a large city high school. The police were drawn from the police department of the same city. The community people represented various interests in the community, particularly in relation to the area served by the high school.

Selection of Staff:

(A) Program Personnel

(1) A program coordinator holding a Ph.D. in Clinical Psychology and experience in Community Psychology.

2) An intern in Community Psychology with experience in sensitivity training and group relations.
3) A professional with expertise in intergroup relations and extensive knowledge of Black problems.
4) A professor of Political Science with extensive experience in developing simulation exercises.

B) Evaluation Personnel

1) A Social Psychologist.
2) An advanced graduate student in Clinical Psychology with experience in group relations and sensitivity training.

Project Functioning:

The intended function of the program staff was to provide the atmosphere and technical assistance to the project participants which would maximize their productivity in reaching the project's stated goals. In addition, the program staff prepared for and generally ran the actual meetings, and served as a source of feedback to the group as a whole concerning the utility of various exercises and the progress being made toward attainment of the group goals.

The evaluation staff had several functions. They were to monitor the activities of both the program staff and the participants and provide feedback to the program staff as to changes in the behavior of both groups. Administration and interpretation of various psychological instruments, at both the beginning and end of the project, was another major function of the evaluation staff, as was the writing of this report. Finally, this group used a variety of methods to query both participants and program staff as to their impressions of the group's progress as the project was in operation.

Since the major focus of this paper is to present the model which was derived from this training project, an extensive description of the actual project will not be given. However, in order to provide some understanding of what took place during these sessions, the following summary of the types of techniques and activities utilized is provided. It may be noted that most of these activities are designed to actively involve the participants in the learning experience, rather than confining them to the role of passive receivers of information.

Activities Utilized in Youth-Authority Project

I. *Discussion Techniques*

Discussion techniques all involve the process of having participants in the workshop talk to each other about issues relevant to confrontation. These may be relatively free-floating, unstructured discussions or may involve varying degrees of situational structure and topic specificity.

   a) Large Group Discussions

These were open discussions on a variety of topics in which all members of the workshop participated. Structure for these sessions was minimal and topics included: What are the causes of confrontation? Who bears responsibility for confrontation? What is the single most important problem leading to confrontation? Topics were generally suggested by staff members, but were agreed upon by the participants. The direction of the discussions was largely under the control of the participants. Staff members intervened occasionally to suggest directions the discussion might take or to highlight specific points.

   b) Small Group Discussions

This exercise was a variant of the large group discussions in which groups of approximately five or six participants were assembled to discuss specific topics. This technique was used to pinpoint some of each subgroup's particular problems in confrontations. An advantage of this method is that it gives members greater opportunity to participate in discussions.

c)   Panel Discussions

In the workshop, this technique was implemented by asking four students to form a panel and discuss the major cause of confrontation before the entire group. Subsequently, other workshop members made comments and asked questions. This has the advantage of a small group discussion and the added feature of allowing others to observe the ongoing process.

d)   Small Group Discussion--Forced Entrance

This is a variation of techniques (b) and (c) in which a small group carried on a discussion in front of the larger group. Here, however, observing members could make comments or ask questions only by entering the smaller group for the duration of the exercise. This tended to eliminate irrelevant and capricious comments from outside and to further involve discussants in the issue at hand.

II.   Role - Playing Techniques

a)   Hypothetical Situations

In this exercise participants were selected and asked to act out a particular role. An example from the workshop was a situation in which participants acted out a classroom scene composed of a teacher and student roles. In this scene the teacher demonstrates a lack of interest in giving students personal attention. This was very successful in emphasizing a point made by students and some teachers during the workshop that teachers often neglect their students. This technique can be used to dramatize opinions and to make the pressures of a given situation salient to those not normally exposed to them.

b) Role Reversals

Participants can be asked to role-play characters who are different from themselves. An example was asking a policeman to act the part of a Black student and a student to play the role of a police officer in a confrontation situation. As with most role-playing situations, this technique allows the players to experience some of the pressures placed on his character by the situation.

c) Observation of Role-Playing

Watching others play out roles can be a useful experience. Either staff members or participants can act the roles, but other members can see the results of the situation. In this workshop, the staff pointed out relevant changes in participant behavior during and after role-playing exercises. Understanding of the situation seems to be improved by this method.

III. Miscellaneous

a) Listening Exercises

This is an exercise which demonstrates people with conflicting viewpoints rarely listen to each other but instead spend their time in a discussion simply supporting their own previous positions. The technique involves setting up a small group discussion composed of participants who are likely to disagree on an issue and having them discuss the issue before the entire group. The staff then points out the ways in which

people failed to listen to each other, eliciting
similar observations from the group at large.
The next step is to try out ways of listening
more effectively to others.

b) *Simulation*

These are copies or abstractions of
actual social processes, usually including some
sort of role assignments. In the workshop, a
game entitled "The Good Society" was devised by
William Coplin and Steven J. Apter.[2] Various
degrees of power and influence were allocated
to several groups of participants through the
rules of the game. These participants were
then assigned a task in which groups competed
for power and influence. The simulation allows
a demonstration of the effects of differential
power and status on the behavior of groups and
individuals. This should lead to a better
understanding of why people behave as they do
in social - political situations.

c) *Forced Field Analysis*

This is a technique developed by the
National Training Laboratory.[3] It was designed
to aid participants in accomplishing various
political and interpersonal goals by analyzing
situational elements which might facilitate or
inhibit goal attainment. Participants were
asked to define a goal or goals which were
relevant to the confrontation situation and then
go list the various obstacles to attainment, as
well as forces (people or things) which would aid
them in attaining these goals. They then were
asked to eliminate items which they could not
influence and develop strategies for minimizing
the obstacles they could affect, as well as to
find ways of using forces which worked their
favor.

d) *Religious Panel*

Two members of the local religious community were invited to make statements concerning their ideas about the nature and causes of confrontation and to reply to questions from the group on that subject.

e) Guest Speakers

Professionals in areas relevant to the confrontation situation spoke to the group in order to supply information that might help workshop participants in their task.

f) Readings

Material was supplied which concerned itself with confrontation or with youth - authority relationships. This gave participants additional information which could be used in the workshop proper.

Evaluation of the Project:

Again, the primary focus of this paper is the resultant model and not the project itself. Taking into account the reactions of the participants, staff and evaluators it might be stated that as a pilot project it accomplished the initial objectives to some extent, but did not produce any significant changes in the schools or general community. The following is an excerpt from the summary of the evaluator's report:

A general evaluation of the project would have to be : it seemed to be effective but it could have been better....
The project was a success if it eliminates or (more realistically) reduces confrontations in the schools. It was a failure if it does not accomplish this goal. There is no way, however, of really knowing which is the real case. For this reason, we looked at the experiences of

and changes in the participants, as well as
the staff's feelings about the project. Notable
changes took place among the participants and there
was a general feeling about the part of all
involved that something was gained through the
project, but not as much as might have been. Only
if the newly gained knowledge is applied by the
people involved to concrete situations will this
project bear the fruit desired. This is still
an empirical question. Recent activity on the
part of participants, although relatively modest,
engenders a moderate degree of optimism that the
project will have a beneficial effect upon the
situation in the schools and that some techniques
were developed that are usable in minimizing the
negative effects of conflict between youth and
those who have authority over them.[4]

Recommendations for a Working Model

After conducting the current project, the
staff met in order to assess the project and to
develop a general model which might be applicable
for a number of youth - authority situations.
We considered our impressions of the project we
had completed, the ideas and reactions supplied
by the participants in our discussions with them,
and the report of the evaluation team. From
these sources we developed some general principles
and strategies which might be used as guidelines
by persons interested in designing programs in
this area. These guidelines would be appropriate
for inservice training programs withing specific
sub-groups, such as police, teachers, students;
they would be relevant for small inter-group
experiences, as in the current project; and
they might be used in situations involving larger
social systems, such as an entire school or
neighborhood. The guidelines may be used in
planning either educational or action oriented
programs.

The recommendations are presented in

general, rather than specific terms, for several
reasons. First, the intent of these suggestions
is to generate programs for many groups and
situations which relate to the issue of confrontation between youth and authority. A specific
recommendation would only be useful for a
particular problem, involving a limited range
of individuals. Also, the activities and
techniques which have been utilized to date have
not been tried and evaluated sufficiently to
guarantee success. Their degree of effectiveness
has not been empirically established. Finally,
it would be presumptuous to prescribe a precise
program for any situation with which we are not
directly familiar. Each group of people is
unique; the problems and assets they possess
vary; and the most suitable approach is rarely
identical for different groups. Only through
direct contact and familiarity with groups can
a specific program be developed. Therefore we
are providing the basic materials and tools
needed to build a program. The exact methods
and plans for developing any particular program
must be determined by those who are responsible
for that project.

Suggested Program Model:

     The proposed model conceptualizes programs
as being divided into three phases. While these
phases would follow in chronological sequence they
would not be totally independent of each other.
There would be some overlap and often it would
be advisable to return to a previous phase when
obstacles arise during an advanced phase. Each
of the phases would consist of a series of
activities directed at enhancing the particular
objectives of that sequence. Some of the
activities might be drawn from those used in
the current project; others might be selected
from outside sources; and still others
might be designed by the planners of

each individual program. The three phases of
this model are:

   1. Improving Communication among
   Participants.
   2. Understanding Conditions and
   Problems which Produce Confrontation.
   3. Developing and Implementing Strategies
   for Alleviating Conditions and Resolving
   Problems which Produce Confrontation.

A brief explanation of each phase is given below:

1. Improving Communications among Participants

     The initial task of any project of this type
is to establish open and honest communication
among the members of the various groups. This
requires refinement of both expressive and
listening behaviors. In some situations, the
participants merely have to be given an opportunity
to become familiar with each other in order to
establish good communication. In other cases,
there are psychological and sociological obstacles
which must be overcome before participants can
communicate effectively. Finally, there are some
instances in which the participants need to
develop the basic communication skills of expressing themselves clearly, and listening attentively
to others. Most programs will probably involve
some conbination of these communication activities:
familiarization, obstacle reduction, and skill
building.

     Improving communication through familiarization
is a relatively simple task. When there are no
serious personal or interpersonal barriers
impeding communication, it may be necessary to
merely place the participants in a situation which
allows them to interact with each other on an
informal basis. Small topic - oriented group
discussions, person-to-person dyads and "bull
sessions" might help to reduce social distance

among participants.

Obstacles impeding communication may be located within individuals or between them. Prejudicial attitudes, defenses engendered by fear and insecurity or inadequate information may prevent a participant from communicating with others. Barriers which exist between individuals include different interests, attitudes, and values, and discrepancies in cultural perspectives. There may be no intrinsic problem with any of the participant's beliefs; it may only be the distance created by the distance which fosters communication difficulties. Activities which focus on participants interacting within spheres of shared interests and experiences and exercises - including guided discussion and role-reversal which enable others to exchange information which increases their understanding of each other's views - are applicable in this area of communication development.

Those situations which require the enhancement of basic communication skills are usually the most time-consuming. Often, fundamental skills must be taught by participants before they can effectively communicate with each other. Role-playing and rehearsal-type activities may assist in improving expressive skills, while "listening" exercises may enhance receptivity.

2. *Understanding Conditions and Problems which Produce Confrontation*

The second phase is directed toward increasing the participants' understanding of the factors and causes related to confrontation. This knowledge may be acquired in a variety of ways. Some of this information may be obtained through direct interaction of the participants (e.g., small and large group discussion). Outside

resources, such as books, films and lectures
may serve as valuable means of transmitting
knowledge. Also, simulations and other
exercises may be designed to facilitate the
understanding process. A final source of
learning is direct experience gained through
field trips and work projects.

All of these activities may potentially
lead to increased awareness and understanding
of the conditions which produce confrontation.
The specific selection and order of presentation
of activities must be made according to the
objectives of the project and the nature of the
people in the program. If the understanding
process becomes impeded during this phase it
may be necessary to revert to the previous
phase and introduce activities which will
improve the communication process.

3. *Developing and Implementing Strategies for
    Alleviating Conditions and Resolving
    Problems which Produce Confrontation*

Developing good communications, and
increasing the level of understanding of
conditions which produce confrontation, are
important objectives. However they are not
sufficient by themselves. To be truly worthwhile, communication and understanding must
generate the development and implementation of
methods for alleviating conditions producing
confrontation.

Activities in this phase would include
anything which relates to the planning and
operation of problem resolution strategies.
Small and large scale programs might be
instituted. Solutions would progress from
discussion activities through direct action.
Short-term as well as long-term projects
would be appropriate. Programs might range
from human relations training to curriculum

changes to school governance revision to ethnic
and cultural activities.

It should be noted that by the time the
third phase is reached, some solution may have
been achieved through improved communication
and understanding. By the same token, communication and understanding will not have been
perfected by that time, and it may be necessary
to revert to communication and understanding
activities if problem resolution is not
proceeding effectively.

Procedural Recommendations

The development of any program in an
area as complex and volatile as confrontation
between youth and authority requires a great
deal of careful planning. Project staff must
be sensitive to the needs of the participants
and the direct and subtle problems connected
with the program. Preparation and implementation
must be done methodically. Each activity should
have its own explicit purpose, and provision
should be made to periodically evaluate the
effectiveness of the program. The following
suggestions are presented to assist persons
who are developing youth - authority
confrontation programs

1. *Representatives from all groups participating
   in the program should be involved in actual
   planning.* When participants are associated
with formal organizations (Teachers' Association,
Students' Organization, Police Benevolence
Association, Board of Education, Civil Rights
groups, etc.) it is important to obtain the
sanction, and if possible, direct involvement
of these groups.

2. *In the selection of participants an effort
   should be made to include members from all
   groups which might relate to the problems*

to be dealt with in the current project.
It is especially important to include persons
in decision-making positions, as well as those
who are directly involved with day-to-day
happenings (e.g., school administrators, as
well as teachers; student leaders, as well as
students who do not occupy "official"
positions). Programs which are intended to
have significant current and future impact
must be thoroughly understood and supported by
persons who are in positions of influence.
Similarly, effectiveness cannot be achieved
without the cooperation of those people
directly affected by it.

3. *The objectives of the program should be
   defined in clear and precise terms, with
   behavorial goals included whenever possible.*
Each objective should be stated in a manner
which allows for assessment of the achievement
of this objective at some later point in time.
Criteria for success should be described in
detail.

4. *Participants and staff should share their
   expectations of the program and should
   reach an explicit agreement on what the
   program's goals and methods will be before
   the program begins.* It is essential that
people thoroughly understand the nature of their
endeavors so that they may voluntarily commit
themselves to participation, with an awareness
of what they are becoming involved in. This
does not mean that everyone must share the
same ideas of desired outcome - - if they did
there would probably be no point in conducting
the program - - but it is necessary that the
basic game and ground rules be agreed upon.

5. *Meetings should be conducted at frequent
   intervals, over a moderate period of time,
   with provision of opportunities for
   additional learning between meetings and*

and follow-up after the conclusion of the
formal program period. Meetings should be
planned so that participants are able to
maintain continuity of substance and spirit
from one meeting to the next without overcrowding
the schedule. Take - home in the form of action
projects, and further learning experiences should
be made available, but not thrust on people in a
manner which will make them associate it with
traditional "homework" assignments given in school.
It is also crucial to continue contact with
participants and their projects after the conclusion
of the formal meeting phase of the project. This
continued contact may vary from checking on the
participant's progress to offering consultative
services and additional resources. Occasionally
a group "reunion" may be useful as a means of
assessing what has happened since the program
terminated.

6. *The purpose and meaning of each activity should*
   be precisely defined and accurately communicated
   to the participants. It is important that
participants understand why they are engaging in
whatever exercise or interaction they are currently
experiencing, and how this activity relates to the
general issues they are addressing. In addition
to presenting a comprehensible rationale before
the activity commences, the participant should be
given an opportunity to discuss the significance
of their experience after it occurs. A new
activity should not be introduced until the
participants have adequately responded to and
comprehend the old one.

7. *There must be continual awareness of the*
   cognitive, affective and behavioral status of
   the participants, and an appropriate balance
   must be maintained among these facets as
   the participants are exposed to change -
   inducing activities. In attempting to work
in such a sensitive and personalized problem -
solving situation, adequate attention must be paid

to all aspects of the individual participant's
functioning.   Some popular misconceptions
in dealing with the issue of confrontation are:
a) insight by itself will lead to problem
resolution; b) a highly charged face-to-face
confrontation is all that is needed; c) if a
person is forced to act appropriately, his
attitude will naturally adjust accoringly. None
of these statements is valid because they are
all based on highly simplistic premises. In
order to create a climate in which individuals
are willing to examine their own attitudes and
behavior, it is necessary to minimize the
element of personal threat, while maximinzing the
incentives for self-awareness and interpersonal
communication. Anxiety will naturally be
induced in a setting which is characterized by
unfamiliar faces and seemingly unpredicable
demands and interactions, but this anxiety must
not be allowed to reach a level which forces
the individual to erect impenetrable defenses.
In the same way, a certain amount of cognitive
awareness will facilitate problem resolution,
but an overemphasis on intellect and the
rational approach can serve as a means of avoid-
ing the real issue. In order to insure progress,
it is necessary to affect all of these modalities:
cognitive, affective and behavioral. Activities
must be timed to maintain a harmonious balance
among the participant's faculties. For instance,
an emotional face-to-face confrontation may be
necessary to enable a participant to focus on a
prejudicial attitude, but a prior atmosphere
of acceptance and trust would need to have been
established to allow the person to feel safe
enough to engage in self-examination. And a
period of rational discussion would have to
follow the confrontation in order to facilitate
understanding and consolidation of the new
awareness.

8. *The program should include a balanced offering
    of confrontative and cooperative type activities.*

At some stages, it may be important to encourage participants to resolve conflicts among themselves through direct confrontation; at other times cooperative activity leading to group cohesiveness will be important to facilitate rapport and mutual understanding among the participants. The selection of a particular activity at any point of development ought to be made on the basis of first-hand information about the level of development of that group.

9. *As the program evolves, the locus of responsibility for program planning and determination should be shifted from the staff to the participants.* While the staff may need to assume a leadership role in order to facilitate the initial phases of the program, the participants must be encouraged to accept responsibility for the program's direction once they are adequately informed about the alternatives available to them. If this shift of responsibility does not occur, the program cannot succeed beyond a minimal level of accomplishment. Staff can function most effectively as a resource for the members, facilitating group interaction, and providing information and alternative approaches when these are requested by the participants.

10. *Honest expression and interaction are necessary for successful problem resolution.* While it would be unrealistic (and perhaps destructive)to have participants express their latent attitudes and innermost feelings at the initial meeting, there should be a strong effort to create a climate in which honesty and openness are encouraged and accepted. For this to occur support must be given to those who risk honest expression. Otherwise, negative reactions to honesty will extinguish any inclination toward desired behavior.

*11   Staff members must model all of the behavior
      which they encourage participants to practice.*
The success of the program will be most dependent
on the staff's ability to express themselves
honestly, react nondefensively to criticism,
always attempt to empathize with others, and work
cooperatively as an effective team. If the
staff expects the participants to behave in
this manner, they must do so themselves.

        The program model and procedural
recommendations which have been presented are
intended to serve as general guidelines for
persons interested in establishing projects in
the area of youth - authority confrontation.

        These principles may be used as a
starting point for program development. They
are not intrinsically valuable. Their value may
be realized when they provide people with guidelines that are used to promote creative and
flexible programs directed at resolving serious
dilemmas. In the last analysis, it is neither
the articulate principles, nor the neat little
activities which insure success; rather, it is
the honest involvement, creative thinking and
dedicated commitment of the participants and
staff which will lead to effective resolution
of the problems which exist between youth
and authority.

FOOTNOTES

1. This paper is based, in part, on a project sponsored by Title I of the New York State Department of Education. A more complete description of the project may be found in the final report submitted to that agency. The report is entitled, *Confrontations: Youth and Authority.*

2. *Confrontations: Youth and Authorities.* Final Report of Project Conducted by the Continuing Education Center for the Public Service in collaboration with The Institute Community Psychology, Syracuse University. Prepared for Title I Office, New York State Education Department, July, 1971.

3. Eisen, S. And Mill, S.R. *A problem-solving program for defining a problem and planning action.* National Training Laboratory Institute for Applied Behavioral Science: Washington, D. C., 1969.

4. *Controntations: Youth and Authorities. op. cit.*

SECTION IV:

ASSESSMENT OF POLICE PERFORMANCE

8. AN EVALUATION OF THE EFFECTS ON CITIZENS' ATTITUDES OF THE CRIME CONTROL EXPERIMENT

Sidney Oglesby, Robert P. Sprafkin,
Robert Cohen and Dennis Angelini

*Whom does the social scientist represent
when working with a police agency? Is it the
administrative body which controls the purse
strings? The police officers? The social
science community? Or the citizens being served
by the police agency? This question needs to
be addressed by the social science practitioner,
prior to reaching a formal working agreement
with a police agency. The manner in which the
practitioner defines his or her sense of
accountability or advocacy will influence the
nature of the work performed and the ways in
which the results will be used. For example,
a consultant who views himself as primarily
accountable to the citizens of the community
would probably choose not to become involved
in an evaluation project which did not allow
for public dissemination of the results, while
another consultant, who sees himself serving
as an agent of the police administrators, might
be more willing to work on such a program.*

*The paper by Sidney Oglesby, et al.
describes an evaluation project in which the
social scientists involved attempted to be
accountable to the citizens of the community*

while fulfilling their responsibilities to the
police and city officials who had requested
their services.   In additon to describing the
methodology of their citizen attitude survey
project, the authors illustrate their contention
that the consultant is usually accountable to
more than one source and in actual practice
it is difficult to maintain an appropriate
balance because of the conflicting interests
expressed by these sources.

In the attitude survey reported in this
paper, the authors were concerned about
increasing police responsiveness to citizens'
expressed needs and attitudes.   The difficulty
they had in achieving this objective is
indicative of the problem inherent in situations
in which the consultant feels accountable to
more than one source.

In recent years the work of police
departments across the country has emerged as
a public issue. Various segments of society
have called for changes, reforms, and innovations
in order for the public to be better served by
more adequate police services. One such attempt,
aimed at providing selected high crime neighborhoods in a middle-sized Northeastern City with
better police coverage is known as the Crime
Control Team (CCT) concept. This chapter presents
an evaluation of citizens' attitudes toward CCT
practices as one index of the overall effectiveness of the experimental project.

Crime Control Teams were developed as
experimental attempts at team policing to
supplement existing police services with
specially trained officers recruited from the
police force. These officers were assigned to
specific geographic sections of the city, known
as CCT areas, and were intended to provide
and be directly responsible for a full range
of police services to resident of those areas.

Crime Control Teams were characterized in terms of their autonomy and their ability to utilize a wide range of skills in order to meet the residents' needs for a broad spectrum of police services. There was an emphasis placed upon the notion of continuity of services within a small team of policemen; of returning to the concept of the neighborhood "cop on the beat" who knows his constituents and who could be called upon in a wide variety of situations.

In order to assess the effectiveness of the CCT in terms of its impact on citizens' attitudes, a two-year evaluation project was undertaken. The design of the project called for a comparison of the attitudes of residents of areas served by the CCT (as well as a control or non CCT area) before and after the institution of CCT service in the neighborhoods (1971-1973). Attitudes were assessed by means of questionnaires administered to representative samples of residents in each of the designated areas. The following section of the chapter describes the means by which this was done, the results of the survey, a discussion and recommendations.

PROJECT DESIGN AND IMPLEMENTATION

Survey Instrument: The means by which citizens' attitudes were assessed involved the development of a survey instrument (questionnaire) dealing with the following areas of concern: 1) "Who would you call?" An attempt at identifying who people call for what services when confronted with various crime and noncrime situations in the neighborhood; 2) Attitudes and feelings about police and police services; 3) Amount of contact and awareness about police and police services; 4) Evaluation of priorities in terms of police services; and 5) Demographic characteristics of the respondents (see Appendix A).

The survey instrument was developed by

the Institute for Community Development and
reviewed by professional consultants, representatives of city government and representatives of
the police department. It was also reviewed by
several prominent members of the CCT neighborhoods
prior to the onset of the survey proper. This
was done to obtain additional feedback on the
appropriateness of the wording and content of
the instrument, and, implicitly, to gain some
degree of community sanction for the study.
These community representatives were paid as
temporary consultants and did not constitute a
permanent board or review committee. Finally,
the instrument was pilot tested (with 208
respondents) in a neighborhood demographically
similar to the CCT areas.

   Surveyors: The interviews for the survey
proper were conducted by 13 interviewers recruited
from the CCT and control neighborhoods. Several
of these interviewers were referred by the
aforementioned community consultants. The chief
of police reserved the right to review the list
of interviewers' names. These residents,
inexperienced in survey and interviewing methods,
were rigorously trained over a nine week period
by a member of the ICD staff.

TRAINING

   Purpose and Potential Payoff: Initial
resistance was dealt with through frank discussions with CCT residents/interviewers concerning
the purposes of the study and potential payoff
to the community. Considerable time was spent
explaining the construction and design of the
instrument and reasons for objective survey
methods. Particular concerns of the interviewers
were with the reasons for obtaining demographic
identification, the importance of insuring
confidentiality and the grouping of data.
Follwing several sessions spent on the above-
mentioned issues, nine three hour sessions

over a four week period were spent in practicing
interview techniques (role playing, feed back,
taping, critiquing). Three of the interviewers
were designated and paid as supervisors and
were responsible for auditing every tenth
interview to insure reliability. Most of the
same interviewers were reemployed for the
post-test survey, and were given a refresher
course in interview methods.

Survey Design and Sample: The study was
initially conceived of as an assessment of
attitudes prior to and after the institution
of CCTs. In actuality, due to the deployment
schedule of the police department, only one of
the two experimental (CCT) districts was a
"pure" pre-test. In the other, the CCT had
already been in operation for a few months prior
to the administration of the pre-test. CCT's
remained in operation at the time of the post
test in both experimental districts.

The actual *pre* survey involved a
stratified sample of 933 persons; approximately
350 in each CCT area and 200 in the control
area. The post survey was administered to 957
demographically similar persons with
approximately the same distribution by
geographic districts. The sampling design
divided the total population into 13 geographi-
cally designated sections. Each interviewer
was responsible for 75 interviews in his
section with a maximum of five per street.

Additional data were analyzed in terms
of pre-post comparisons around the demographic
variables of race/ethnicity, age, sex, length of
a residence, penal experience, etc.

RESULTS AND RESIDENTS' RECOMMENDATIONS

Some of the results and community
residents' recommendations emerging from

analysis of the pre and post comparisons of the data are:

1)   *"Who Would You Call?"* For the total sample there was an increase (pre to post) in willingness to call police for a variety of concerns. In the post test as compared with the pre test, respondents in all areas indicated they would call the police for help for a wider variety of problems. The exception to this trend was in the area of drug use and sale, where there was a decrease in willingness to contact police. The respondents in the control area expressed a willingness to call police in a much wider range of situations than respondents in either experimental district (pre to post increases in 17 out of 21 situation in the control area versus increases in 6 out of 21 and 9 out of 21 situations in the two experimental areas).

2)   *Attitudes toward Police* Attitudes toward police were assessed by means of a 26 item Likert - type scale, with a five point range of response for each item (1=most positive; 5-most negative). Thus, the lower the mean score, the more positive the attitude. A neutral response (3) on all items would yield a score of 78. Scores toward police in all three districts became more positive over the period of the study, with the greatest change occurring in the control district (see Table 1). Black attitudes became more positive in both control and experimental districts, with the greatest change occurring in the control area. In all areas, White attitudes at the end of the study were more positive than Black attitudes (see Table 2).

TABLE 1:   Comparison of Mean Attitude Toward Police in Three Districts,Pre and Post

MEAN ATTITUDE

		Pre	Post
	Control	73.99	67.67
DISTRICT	E_2	75.79	72.41
	E_1	76.11	72.54

TABLE 2: Comparison of Mean Attitude Toward Police in Three Districts as a Function of Ethnicity, Pre and Post

		MEAN ATTITUDE	
		Pre	Post
Control	Black	76.0	68.6
	Other	69.9	64.8
	White	67.1	64.6
District	Black	78.7	73.7
E_2	Other	72.1	61.6
	White	68.6	65.6
District	Black	78.4	75.0
E_1	Other	75.2	67.3
	White	69.2	66.1

Some of the other attitudinal findings were:
a) There was no clear relationship found between the frequency of seeing police in the neighborhood and attitudes toward police.
b) When viewed in terms of sex/ethnicity/age, all groups, with the exception of teenage Black males, tended to become less negative over time.
c) Those respondents with previous penal experience or experience in detention homes reported negative attitudes toward police, which did not change over time.

3) Awareness of CCT Residents in all districts reported an increased awareness of the existence of CCT's over the period of the study.

4) Contact with Police There was a small pre-to-post increase in the two experimental areas in the number of residents who reported

that they personally knew policemen. There was
a decrease in reports of such personal knowledge
in the control district. Across all groups,
the majority of the respondents indicated that
they did not personally know any policemen.

   5) Recommendations about Police Services
Respondents in both experimental districts
increased substantially in their endorsement of
the necessity for changes in police service.
Although a majority of respondents in the control
district also expressed this endorsement in the
pre test, the result of the post test indicated
a decrease in a willingness to endorse the need
for changes in police service. In both experimental
districts, respondents expressed increased dis-
agreement (pre-to-post) with the recommendation
that more policemen were needed in the neighborhood.
Other recommendations for police services that
received endorsement were primarily in the areas
of social and recreational services.

DISCUSSION

     During the contract negotiations for the
CCT study the researchers were very concerned
about the cost/benefit to the community which was
to be studied. Essentially, to conduct the study
would depend upon a tremendous amount of cooperation
from the respondents of this lower socio-economic
level community. ICD felt an obligation to insure
that this community would receive some benefits
for their cooperation in the process of the study
in terms of some immediate direct returns from the
results of the study.

     Consequently, by prior agreement, the
results were to be submitted to city officials,
the police department, and after 60 days would be
made available to the news media as a vehicle for
disseminating the information back to the
community. The assumption underlying this process
was that we, as social scientitsts, had an

obligation, not only to be objective in our
research methodology, but also a responsibility
to reinforce the credibility of social science
in the community being studied by demonstrating
some payoff to the community. The vehicle in
this study for demonstrating such a payoff was
the dissemination of the results to the news
media, and the distribution of recommendations
to all interested parties, including active
civic organizations not associated with the
study. The implicit assumption was that the
provision of accurate information to the public
would lead to recommended changes, and hence
some desired payoff to the community.

However, after one year since the
release of the information, the payoff to the
community studied has been minimal in terms of
visible changes in police practices. The payoff
for us as social scientists has been mixed: An
interesting and competent research project, but
yet another example of no visible effect on
social policy or community life. The payoff to
city officals and the police is less clear. Funds
have been brought into the city and positive
attention has been focused on the innovative
efforts of the police! However, none of the
positive attention has incorporated our findings
or the recommendations stemming directly from
community residents.

Perhaps this is a fortunate circumstance,
since it forces us, as social scientists, to
re-evaluate our roles in research supported by
public monies while having no viable vehicles
established to insure some public benefit. As
social scientists we would no doubt be able to
continue indefinitely to turn out competent,
encapsulated research. However, we feel that
it is time to examine the focus of our efforts
and priorities. We believe that future efforts
by social scientists should be directed toward
the issues of implementation: Who do you work

for, who are you responsible to, what will happen
to the information, can you be assured that results
will receive appropriate exploration and possible
action? In short, what is called for is making
explicit the public responsibilities of social
scientists involved in community issues.

Our feeling about the relationship
between police and social scientists in the
evaluation project described above is that much
was lost by not making explicit ˙ the expectations
of each group before agreeing to enter into the
project. It appeared as if the police viewed
the social scientists as their agents, whose
product could be used or not, depending on the
needs of the agent. These were clearly not our
expectations as social scientists. In retrospect,
we find ourselves feeling used, indignant,
ineffectual, ignored. While we did insist on
presenting our results to the news media after
60 days, we realize that this alone was an
insufficient method for insuring that the results
of a publicly financed study would be acted upon.
In short, as social scientists working with
police, we feel as if we never adequately forced
ourselves or the police to come to grips with
the issues of accountability and responsiveness.
Our mandates were only to present competent
research. The police and city government were
bound by no specific mandate, other than to allow
the findings to be published.

While we may bask in the wisdom and/or
discomfort of hindsight, we must admit that we have
no adequate solutions to the issues of responsiveness
and accountability. What appears as a reasonable
possibility, however, is to establish a responsible,
representative, and enfranchised advisory committee
to monitor the implementations and response to such
public - funded projects. Such a committee,
perhaps composed of police, city officials,
community residents, etc. could be given the

mandate to investigate and implement the recommendations emerging from community - based projects. The present study highlights one fact: Recommendations are not implemented authomatically. Indeed, there may have been public reactions, but such reactions, without built in mechanisms for change, seem little more than futile cries.

APPENDIX A

CCT SURVEY INSTRUMENT

Part I.

"We are interested in finding out who people in this neighborhood call when they are seeking help in different situations. I am going to read you a list of problem situations and I would like you to tell me who, if anyone, you would call for each case. For example, if the problem was a fire in your home, you might call the fire department.

I'll read each situation and you tell me who you would call for help. If you wouldn't call anyone, just say 'no one.'"

Write answer or No One
Give Name
Who would you first call about

1. eviction notice..........................
2. neighbor's fight (overheard or seen)......
3. neighbor has heart attack................
4. see shoplifting..........................
5. fight in own family......................
6. cars illegally parked in street..........
7. hear gunfire.............................
8. see drug sale............................
9. see drug use.............................
10. property damage to your home.............
11. if you were involved in an auto accident..
12. street lights out........................
13. abandoned car............................
14. fight in school..........................

15. complaint against local storeowner.......
16. complaint against city agency...........
    (welfare, housing, etc.)
17. complaint about police harassment........
18. your child not behaving in school........
19. complaint against landlord..............
20. problem with your neighbor..............
21. rioting.................................

Part II.

"Now I'm going to read you some statements about peoples' feelings and attitudes toward the police. I would like you to tell me, for each one, how you feel about the statement. Whether you strongly agree, agree, are undecided, disagree, or strongly disagree. (Give respondent separate card with choice alternative listed). Please choose one of these (point to alternatives) for each statement.

strongly agree   agree   undecided   disagree   stongly
                                                 disagree
Answer

_____1.   police are always around when you need them.

_____2.   Policemen should be paid more money for
           the job they do.

_____3.   Policemen enjoy pushing people around.

_____4.   Policemen are very important in preventing
           crime in this neighborhood.

_____5.   The police push people around more in this
           neighborhood than any other parts of the
           city.

_____6.   Policemen in this neighborhood try real
           hard to be helpful.

_____7.   In this neighborhood more than others a
           policeman has to be tough to do his job.

_____8.   Most policemen are pretty nice guys.

_____9.   Of all the people in the city, the people in this neighborhood get the worst deal from the police.

_____10. Policemen in this neighborhood don't use force unless they have to.

_____11. Most of the people in this neighborhood believe that policemen are pigs.

_____12. I hate to be seen talking with a policeman.

_____13. Policemen in this neighborhood are willing to help with problems other than crime.

_____14. Policemen are changing for the better.

_____15. People in this neighborhood respect the police.

_____16. Policemen need the support of people in the neighborhood in order to do their job.

_____17. I would help the police.

_____18. More innocent people are arrested in this neighborhood than in other parts of the city.

_____19. There seems to be more of a real need for police in this neighborhood than in other parts of the city.

_____20. People in this neighborhood trust the police.

_____21. Policemen in this neighborhood don't understand the people who live here.

_____22. People in this neighborhood are afraid of the police.

____23.   Policemen are prejudiced.

____24.   People arrested by the police in this
          neighborhood are usually guilty.

____25.   Most policemen do their job as best they
          can.

____26.   There is more crime in this neighborhood
          than in most other parts of the city.

____27.   My own feelings about the police are very
          similar to the feelings of most people
          in this neighborhood.

____28.   I am very satisfied with the police
          service in my neighborhood.

Part III.

        "Now I want to ask you some questions about
your own contact with the police."

1.   How often do you usually see policemen on your
      street: (circle one)

a. Less than   b. once or twice   c. every other day
   once a week   a week

d. once a day   e. several times a day

2.   About how many different policemen do you see
      in your neighborhood in a week's time?

a. none   b. 1-2   c. 3-5   d. 6-10   e. 11-20
f. over 21   g. don't know

3.   Do the policemen in your neighborhood all wear
      the same color shirts?

a. Yes___   b. no___
a. what color   1. white 2. blue 3. grey
                 4. all colors 5. don't know

4. Are most policemen in your neighborhood

	yes	no	don't know
a. in all white cars?	___	___	_____
b. in unmarked cars?	___	___	_____
c. on motor cycles?	___	___	_____
d. on foot	___	___	_____
e. in black & white cars?	___	___	_____

circle one

5. How often do the policemen in your neighborhood
   speak to you?
   a. never b. seldom c. sometimes d. often e. very
   often
6. How oten do you talk to a policeman in your
   neighborhood?
   a. never b. seldom c. sometimes d. often e. very
   often
7. Do you personally know any of the policemen in
   your neighborhood?
   a. none b. yes, but no number given c. 1-2 d.3-5
   e. more than 5

8. Have you ever called the police? yes__ no____
   (If no, go to Section IV)
9. When was the last time you called the police?

a. within last 2 weeks   d. within last 6 months
b. within last month   e. within last year
c. within last 3 months   f. over 1 year ago

10 If yes to above

a. how *soon* did they come the last time you called
   them?

1. never arrived 2. more than hour later
3. less than 1 hour later 4. very helpful

b. how helpful were they?
1. not helpful 2. somewhat helpful 3. helpful
4. very helpful

Part IV.

1. "The following suggestions about police services, police work and crime protection have been made by people in the neighborhood. I would like you to tell me how you feel about each one; whether you strongly agree, agree, are undecided, disagree, or strongly disagree. (Give respondent separate cards with choice alternatives and suggestions listed). Please choose one of these,point to alternatives, for each statement." Read suggestions aloud.

Answer____ 1. more policemen in neighborhood
____ 2. more black policemen in neighborhood
____ 3. more citizens' control of police
____ 4. more police involvement in community activities
____ 5. more informal contact with police
____ 6. fewer policemen in neighborhood
____ 7. more policemen on foot
____ 8. policemen as coaches for sports activities with youth
____ 9. policemen meet informally with neighborhood people - coffee hours,etc.
____ 10. policemen attend meetings of neighborhood groups - church groups, PTA, etc.
____ 11. policemen attend neighborhood social events
____ 12. more policemen live in neighborhood
____ 13. policemen spend more time with problems other than crimes - family problems, school problems, etc.
____ 14. policemen sponsor social events.
____ 15. crackdown on drug sales
____ 16. crackdown on drug users
____ 17. crackdown on gambling and numbers
____ 18. better riot control
____ 19. crackdown on prostitution
____ 20. more policemen in and around schools
____ 21. crackdown on vagrancy and loitering
____ 22. no changes necessary

"Do you have any other suggestions about police services, police work or how police should handle crime that you feel are important but not included on this list? if so, what are they?"

2. Give me one word which you feel best describes policemen

_____

3. Have you ever heard Police Department Crime Control Team (CCT)?
   yes_____no_____

Part V. Classification Information

"As I mentioned earlier, this information will be completely confidential. However, in order to give the information back to the general public, we have to organize it.
   I would like to ask you some classification questions, it would be extremely helpful if you would answer them the best you can."

1. sex: Male_____   female____how old are you?___

2. Education - what was the last year you completed in school (circle 1)

1 2 3 4 5 6 7 8 9 10 11 12 13 14 15 16 16+

3. What's your family (ethnic and racial) background? _____

4. How many children are there in the household under school age? _____
   elementary school (how many)_____
   junior high school_____
   senior high school_____

5. How long have you lived at your present address?

   a. 0-6 mo.   c. 1-3 yr.
   b. 6 mo. -1 yr.   d. 3-5 yr.

e. 5-10 yr.   f. over 10 yr.

6. Where did you live before that (street or
   other city)?_____

7. Where are you from originally (state or city)?

8. What do you usually do for a living (job title)?

9. What type of business is it?_____

10. Are you employed full-time_____part-time___
    or unemployed_____

11. Where is your work located? (section of city)
    (circle one)

a. east b. west c. north d. south e. outside f. other

12. Have you ever been arrested? yes___ no_____

13. Have you ever spent time in jail? Yes___no___

14. Have you ever spent time in a detention home
    for youth?
    yes_____ no_____

9. APPLIED BEHAVORIAL ANALYSIS AND THE POLICE: SOME IMPLICATIONS FOR A COMMUNITY RELATIONS TRAINING PROGRAM

Paul T. Harig and John D. Burchard

Applied behavioral analysis is a social science tool which has gained considerable visibility during the last few years. Advocates of this strategy emphasize its value as a program development, as well as an evaluation approach, which increases precision and objectivity of measurement. Paul T. Harig and John D. Burchard propose that behavioral analysis may be effectively used in the development of police-community relations programs. They describe a system that would enable program developers to clearly define their objectives, easily measure what is being done, and effectively evaluate the impact of their program.

One of the major themes of the Harig and Burchard chapter is that evaluation procedures must be built into police programs at the time of the initial planning. Social scientists may make a significant contribution to improving police services if they are able to assist police agencies in developing sophisticated, yet practical evaluation processes which allow for an adequate assessment of community relations and crisis intervention programs.

148

In the past few years we have seen an
impressive flow of federal money going to local
police departments through the Safe Streets Act.
The most popular funding categories have
consistently boosted municipal budgets for
communications, detection and transportation.
Looking back over these "hardware years," we
find a period of law enforcement merchandising
that has included every aspect of technical
sophistication from radar to computers.

The frenzy to secure this technology has
not ordinarily promoted systematic planning or
evaluation of new law enforcement approaches.
In the words of James Vorenberg, former scientific
advisor to President Lyndon Johnson's Commission
on Law Enforcement and the Administration of
Justice, "Our system of crime control is an
unplanned product of history, and shows this
fact plainly (Vorenberg, 1966)."

We are now at a critical point - confronted
by rising crime rates we have increased our law
enforcement manpower by surrounding it with
technology; yet we look out beyond the men and
equipment and see the crime statistics growing.
Where, then do we go from here?

There is ever-growing support for two
aspects of the crime control issue: prevention,
and community development. These factors are
receiving the attention of police departments
in the form of human relations programs and may
become the backbone of the second generation of
crime control. However, many local departments
will be sailing in uncharted waters when trying
to implement such programs. They are faced with
vague and ill defined objectives such as "developing
officers who can effectively relate with others."
Without a clear definition of purpose, these
police departments risk considerable amounts of
wasted energy. The best programs, on the other
hand, will be those which are more systematic,

and relevant to local needs.

We believe that psychology can make a
positive and supportive response to these
problems of law enforcement training. The
reason for this enthusiasm is the growing
participation of psychologists in applied
research, and the development of a powerful
research methodology derived from the principles
of learning and known as *applied behavior
analysis*. This strategy which is both systematic
and evaluative, has been widely and successfully
demonstrated in areas ranging from education
to rehabilitation, Moreover, the techniques
of behavior analysis are so straightforward
that they can be easily implemented without
an extensive technical background in either
psychology or applied science.

In the following discussion, we will
briefly outline the main features of applied
behavior analysis and conclude with an example
from our own research which pertains to training
techniques for police officers who work with
juveniles.

Applied behavior analysis is a strategy
for finding answers to questions and solutions
to problems (Birnbrauer, et al., 1969). It
has been described as "a self-examining, self-
evaluating, discovery-oriented research procedure
for studying behavior (Baer et al., 1968)."

We often hear complaints that psychology
is too vague or abstract, too caught - up in
theory to offer positive solutions to the
problems of living. Our methods were developed
on the belief that science can be applied to
improve real life situations and that the
effects of all intervention programs can be
defined and measured in such a way as to get
good general agreement on the outcomes.
Behavior analysis really represents a change

in style. Traditionally, we psychologists have
asked questions like, "Why is he doing that?"
We are finally asking "What is he doing....
What can be done to improve it?"

Dealing with what's going on usually
involves three basic operations: to target,
to count, and to intervene. These procedures
are at the heart of every applied behavior
analysis.

Targeting means defining your problems
in ways that you can count or record. It means
taking a very practical look at the situation
to find those *behaviors* which characterize
the problem: some which may need to be
strengthened, some which may need to be
reduced or eliminated. We assume that meaningful changes in these target behaviors will
represent improvement in our problem situation.
The behavior analyst tries to avoid general
labels or global concepts, notions such as
"poorly motivated," "not working to ability,"
"hard to handle,""too defensive," etc. These
labels usually do not offer anything but
confusion when one is trying to define the
problem in tangible or measurable terms. On
the other hand, there are many possible
behaviors which can be found to characterize
the situation.

For example, "being able to relate" can
be translated into a variety of situations in
which the police officer deals with members
of the community, such as occasions when he
encounters a group of kids on the streetcorner.
Whether or not he initiates any conversation,
how long he spends with the youngsters, the
amount of his praise or positive statements
to the kids - these are all measurable aspects
of "relating." One might want to increase his
positive interaction (conversations, praise,
etc.) and decrease other kinds of behaviors

which might occur in the situation, such as the number of questions he asks of the youth, critical comments or warnings, etc. It might also be practical to examine the officer's responses to baiting or unfriendly comments from the youngsters. In this case, we could target the officer's "relating" as the number of angry responses he makes to disrespectful kids. Each of these targets is much more useful and specific in determining the need for a training program than simply going on the hunch that "some of our officers need to get along better with youth."

The kinds of targets we select can lead us to situations for conducting training programs. For example, a program built on the target, "time spent with youth," might suggest some on-the-job intervention to increase an officer's contact with youngsters. The target, "gets angry when criticized" might better be handled in a simulated training experience where we could control the rate of unfriendly remarks directed to the policeman.

The second key operation is *counting*, because this provides the most direct method for determining the strength of the behaviors that are targeted. In general, the ways to measure and record behavioral events consists of determining the frequency of the target behaviors over time.

From a practical, as well as a teaching standpoint, we have found it advisable to encourage people to learn how to count, or monitor, their own behaviors. This method produces the most consistent effects, because the individual learns how to recognize certain features of his behavior and how impose controls. Moreover, this strategy eliminates the impractical step of assigning an observer or impartial rater to follow the individual around during the day.

One problem which might occur at the beginning of such a training program is that the individuals may need to learn how to recognize instances of certain behaviors. For example, in a program which might deal with two target behaviors - positive and negative contacts with youth - an officer might quickly learn how to score some negative encounter, yet be unable (or less able) to recognize certain positive interactions with kids because they are so infrequent, or because he is so accustomed to negative interactions. One method for training officers to recognize positive behaviors might include role playing and studying videotaped models. This would eventually lead to a more reliable identification of various situations.

The next step would be to establish some routine method of looking out for, and scoring the occurrence of the targeted behavior. A check mark in a small notebook is a sufficient system for most behavior analysis projects. Other situations may also include a notation of the time during which the behavior occurred.

Behavior analysts routinely make graphs to record their data, in order to provide direct and practical ways to assess the effect of their interventions.

As an example of the various strategies to measure a target, let's analyze a policeman's conversational behavior with kids. The obvious way to get at this would be to encourage the officer to make a note of his positive contacts. These could be periodically graphed to produce a reasonably accurate estimate of his daily routine. Figure 1 shows sample data for this method.

Another technique would be to encourage

the police officer to make as many contacts
with youngsters as he felt he could without
jeopardizing his efficiency, then record the
time elapsed from his last contact. Charted,
this could serve as a reasonable estimator of
the strength of our officer's sociability.
A sample of the data is presented in Figure 2.

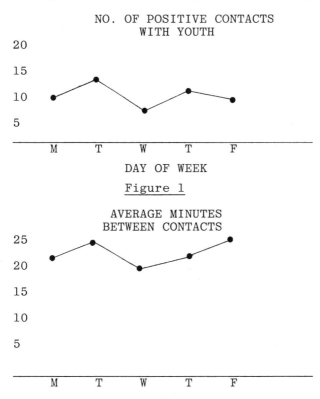

NO. OF POSITIVE CONTACTS
WITH YOUTH

DAY OF WEEK

Figure 1

AVERAGE MINUTES
BETWEEN CONTACTS

Figure 2

AVERAGE LENGTH OF CONTACT
MINUTES

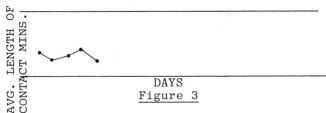

DAYS

Figure 3

AVG. LENGTH OF CONTACT MINS.

A third system of measuring his social behavior could be to request the officer to periodically review his contacts with kids over a normal day at half hour intervals, and to record approximately how long he met with any of them during the observation period. This would provide data on his rate of contact with youngsters. A sample of this type of measurement is provided in Figure 3.

Each of these techniques could provide information on various aspects of our officer's social behavior and could answer specific questions pertaining to relevant targets for him; namely, increasing his interactions with juveniles, prolonging their duration, etc. The advantage of each system depends, to some extent, on the particular question to be answered about the target behavior.

Intervention, the third operation of behavior analysts, relates to their desire to improve the situation under study. One procedure is called"consequating", because it utilizes a simple principle demonstrated repeatedly in the laboratory and observed universally in everyday life: the consequences of any behavior have a profound effect on its occurrence. The pleasant or *rewarding consequences* of a person's behavior tend to strengthen it, while unpleasant or *nonrewarding consequences* weaken or suppress it. The goal of the behavior analyst is to arrange those environmental relationships which are most likely to favor and encourage adaptive behaviors that result in a solution to the problem situation.

Improvements in some situations occasionally call for new behaviors not presently performed by the individual. Reading, for example, is certainly a practical solution to illiteracy but not one which simply occurs by itself in a way that reading could be taught by simply providing the person with a book and hoping that favorable consequences would maintain his progress. Often it is necessary to set up situations which facilitate, or *prompt*, the behavior or even small approximations of it. By prompting, the behavior analyst means to arrange the environment so that it will be maximally conducive to the kinds of behaviors he wants to teach. Study skills, for example, are best learned in favorable situations, e.g., comfortable places which are well lit but undistracting. To place students in such settings would be to provide prompts to encourage, or make more likely, the behaviors such as attention, which are at the heart of good study habits. Another example of a prompt would be to make extra trashcans available when trying to teach antilittering behavior. Occasionally, many prompts occur in controlled or artificial settings. Classrooms or training meetings which attempt to teach skills useful "on the job" are good examples of the use of prompts being employed where the intent is to simulate real - life situations by gradually shaping those skills useful in the natural setting.

The examples which follow illustrate the three basic operations of applied behavior analysis - targeting, counting, and intervening. A word of explanation: rather than dwell on examples already presented in the various publications of education, medicine, and social science, we felt it would be appropriate to

look to the everyday problems of police work,
despite the fact that this area has not yet seen
any applications of applied behavior analysis.
Thus, the following examples are all hypothetical,
although they shall draw on well-documented
principles and techniques, as applied to other
fields. To reiterate, the behavior analyst
targets his problem as a set of behaviors,
provides for a method of counting their strength
or frequency, and makes changes in the target
by arranging the environmental consequences of
the behavior.

Several terms go very well with applied
behavior analysis. The first is obviously
systematic. One of the most appealing features
of this approach is the emphasis on precisely
defined and measureable targets. The behavior
analyst specifies base rates for the observed
behaviors, states in precise terms what the
intervention is, and objectively notes the
accompanying changes in behavior. A potential
situation in which a systematic approach is
useful, might be to increase the amount of time
that patrolmen spend interacting with citizens.
Let's refer to a middle - sized town in which
the crime rate is not unduly large, such that
a typical day's work may include several brief
investigations into relatively minor complaints,
but a large proportion of an officer's time is
consumed by routine cruising in his squad car.
Our target might be to increase the time spent
out of the car, talking with people. This may
be counted as the ratio of time - in versus
time - out, as measured by a number of observations
on his behavior throughout the day. This system
may employ observers, or utilize an officer's
daily log of all transactions with citizens,
or both.

In his initial baseline period, we would
want to encourage the officer to count the
frequency of his daily contacts with regular

citizens. His observations might confirm with
hard data our suspicion that a large portion of
the patrolman's day is spent in the squad car.
Let us assume that our officer made ten
observations daily, which could be routinely
recorded.

The baseline portion of Figure 4 represents
the hypothetical record of incar cruising as a
percentage of the spot checks sampled. In this
case, over 70 percent of the officer's activity
is spent in his car.

Two interventions may be evaluated in
situations such as this. In the first place, one
might want to reduce the officer's proportion of
time spent in his cruiser, assuming that this
would be a first step in increasing the likelihood
that the officer would spend more time among
people. Of course, there are many alternatives
to interacting with people, once the officer has
made the transiton from squad car to street -
for example, standing on the street corner, or
looking "visible" as he strolls alone. For this
reason, an important phase of the intervention
would be to actually increase the frquency of the
officer's citizen contacts, once he is accessable
to them. This would be the second phase of the
sequence.

To accomplish the first intervention, the
behavior analyst may employ a series of prompts
to lower the ratio of car to street activity.
To prompt the officer, making citizen contacts
most likely to occur, he may use several strategies.
First, he might discuss the general desirability
of improved person-to-person exposure: for good
community relations, effective law enforcement,
etc. He could provide the officer with a portable
radio transceiver, making it unnecessary to
remain in his car to be contacted. He may suggest
that the officer concentrate on populated areas,

and that he occasionally park his car and walk.

Figure 4a illustrates hypothetical
results of two possible interventions,
introduced systematically over two successive
periods in order to assess their impact. In
our example, we see that providing the officer
with the equipment to free him from his vehicle
did not necessarily cause him to spend more time
out of it (this hypothetical case is actually
typical of many situations in which prompts do
not, of themselves, cause behavior change,
unless some consequences of the person's environment are also applied to influence it). However,
our suggestions were followed, and they do appear
to have made some effect on the patrolman's out-
of-car behavior. In actual practice, we would
have probably been more rigorous in determining
what effects our initial interventions had, but
these examples suffice for our present discussion.

In the second phase of our intervention,
we are actually dealing with another target -
person-to-person contact. Having increased the
likelihood that the officer would be on the
street, we are seeking to make it more probable
that this time would be filled with contacts with
citizens. For this reason our targets are shifted
to his interpersonal behavior, and our baseline
observations begin again, as illustrated in
Figure 4b, in terms of the percentage of street
behavior in which the officer is observed interacting with a civilian. Our hypothetical case
reveals that the officer was initially observed
at a relatively low level of contacts (less than
20% of the observed intervals). The graph also
presents data on two possible interventions.
Assuming that instructions, which worked successfully to draw the policeman from his squad car,
might again be useful, we might first exhort
the officer to spend more time with people. In
our case, this intervention had a very small
effect. In the second phase, we might add some

favorable consequence when the officer is
observed interacting with a citizen, or a role-
playing session in which he practices various
kinds of interaction; praising him with
enthusiasm, for example. As expected, this
intervention has relatively more success in
achieving our goal for the police officer.

It is certainly possible to elaborate on
this project, refining our interventions to
deal with "friendly" versus "official" citizen
contacts, etc. One of the advantages of applied
behavior analysis is that these rather complex
tasks can be looked at as chains of behavior,
focused on step-by-step to attain the terminal
goal.

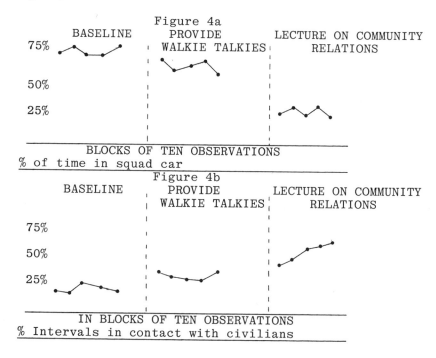

Another complementary term is *evaluation*.
By reason of its practical orientation and its
constant reference to the data, applied behavior
analysis becomes a method by which programs can
be directly assessed in terms of the observable
changes they produce in the target behaviors.
Too often, evaluations are after-the-fact
definitions of what should have occurred. By
contrast, applied behavior analysis allows ongoing
determination of a program's effects. In the
first place, the method defines a program in terms
of operations. It seeks measurable targets and
precise formulations of the expected results of
the program. The programs formulated from applied
behavior analysis often take on a systems analysis
aspect: where program objectives are people -
centered, the terminal goals get defined as
changes in particular target behaviors of a
specified population, with intermediate objectives
defined to obtain those changes. The success of
the program is determined by measuring the amount
of change produced in these targets. Ongoing
measurements are an intrinsic aspect of the
program, with graphs being plotted to constantly
monitor and define its progress. A most useful
advantage of this approach is that evaluative
decisions can be made early in the operational
stages, wherein alternative intervention strategies
can by systematically applied to assess their
comparative effects. Finally, the overall impact
of the program can be determined in a functional
manner, in which it becomes less critical to know
whether the program was a success or a failure
because the developer has information on the
strengths or weaknesses of the individual components
and their relative contribution to the whole
picture.

Applied behavior analysis is also *growth
oriented* because it can be used to document and
direct the ways in which people affect each other's
behavior. In this respect, the police officer
is not only a respondent to a fixed social

situation - he has the opportunity to change the likelihood of certain encounters with the people with whom he interacts.

For example, if we return to our example of the street-corner policeman who meets the same group of youngsters day after day, we have the basis for an effective intervention by that officer. We would begin by targeting two sets of behaviors. Negative contacts between the policeman and the youth could include behaviors such as hostile remarks, for example, kids referring to the policeman as "pig", and occasions of the kids backing away from the officer without anything being said. A more desirable state of events would be one in which the youth smiled, greeted the officer, and exchanged pleasant words of conversation. We would target these as positive behaviors.

As a second step, we would teach the officers how to identify certain exchanges as either positive or negative contacts. They might play-out certain scenes or whatch simulations on videotape. Having learned this, they would begin to take "baseline" counts on the number of occurrences of positive and negative interactions with the group of youngsters during their typical day.

During the intervention phase, we would teach the officers to "shape" the youngsters' behavior. A friendly greeting on the policeman's part could serve as a prompt, and thereby set the occasion for more conversation and a pleasant encounter with the youth. The officer could also try to increase the frequency of the youths' smiles and eye contact through praise and smiles on his own part. As he was learning, each officer would be encouraged to practice those methods and continue to collect data.

Figure 5 illustrates some expected results
of this type of approach. During the intervention
phase, the amount of positive contacts is seen
to steadily increase. This finding, although
not yet explicitly demonstrated between police
officers and youth, has been shown to exist in
enough situations as to be a fairly predictable
result of providing favorable consequences for
social behavior.

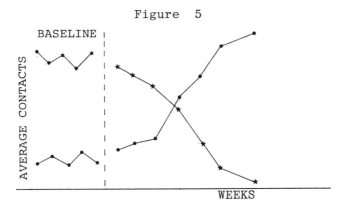

Figure 5

The results of this behavior analysis
could powerfully demonstrate to the person that
his own behavior can be used as an effective
consequence to influence the behavior of others,
e.g., showing that his attention is, after all,
a very useful intervention device.

There are many other situations in day-to-
day police work where an officer has the opportunity
to influence behavior through his attention or
praise. Consider a hypothetical encounter with
several youth who usually gathered near a store
front or on a streetcorner. Their behavior
could probably be caracterized as non-constructive
or "hanging-around" or lazy. Our previous examples
offer some possible alternatives to action. What

happens if the officer chooses to focus his
attention on these non-contructive responses?
It is obviously possible through threat or force
to get the youth to disperse. But is this an
appropriate target? Does our intervention make
it less likely that they will be standing around
doing nothing in the future? Why? It is perhaps
because we would have missed an opportunity to
build constructive responses. What are some of
the alternatives? Based on our examples, we
would suggest that the officer select some
behaviors which are considered incompatible with
"hanging around" - perhaps discussing their
opinions on some issue, about the news, sports,
etc. We would encourage him to give increased
attention to these behaviors, and to follow their
occurrence with interest, warm praise, and
attention. It may, in many cases, be necessary
for him to prompt some of these behaviors, by
asking for the youths' opinions on subjects.
We would predict that in a short time he could
produce a lively, interested group of youngsters,
contrasted to their earlier behavior. In turn,
he could direct their energies to newer activities,
managing a part time job agency, etc. His effort
would probably be less than the repeated energy
and aggravation of moving kids on.

Often these skills have to be developed.
It is not always a comfortable situation to
initiate conversation with a youngster, particularly if he is somewhat hostile or reticent. We are
currently investigating ways to improve these
skills in officers in Vermont, through a behavior
analysis of their interaction behavior with youth
in an interview survey situation.

At the onset, we anchored our training
goals - teaching officers to "relate" to youth -
on these practical tasks: the ability to get a
youth to answer questions, supply information,
and to express his opinions freely. We felt

that this was a satisfactory way to characterize
our objectives. In the first place, we assumed
that an officer who is unable to get a youth to
express his opinions will have considerable
difficulty on "deeper" levels of rapport, whatever
these may be. Further, these behaviors had the
most immediate practical value for police
officers in Burlington, Vermont.

To obtain measurable target behaviors for
these goals, we broke police-juvenile interview
behavior into three areas: *questioning* behavior
which pertains to the interviewer; *answering*
behavior, that pertains to the youth; and the
various *interaction effects* that relate to their
joint behaviors.

Our next procedure was to establish a
setting in which we could obtain a sample of
interview behavior as it existed for each officer,
prior to training. We decided to incorporate
an experimental design which would allow us to
make some exploratory comparisons between police
officers and other types of interviewers, and
between youth with prior police contact and those
with none. We reasoned that if there was any
significant contrast, it would probably occur
between officers and college students who
participate in a Big Brother program; and between
model students and so-called "predelinquents."
Thus, we recruited police and youth-workers on
a task that was camouflaged as a "Youth Opinion
Survey." In a standardized manner, interviewers
would be asked to "try to obtain as much
information as possible from the youth you are
interviewing" on a variety of preselected issues:
school, runaways, police, drugs, religion, after-
school activities, etc. These questions would
be distributed between an officer-youth pair,
so that each youngster could be interviewed twice.
The youth were drawn from two samples: boys
with a prior history of juvenile complaints to
the police, and outstanding students selected

by a guidance personnel at their school and
later screened for previous police contact.
The boys were told that could earn $5 through
being interviewed by someone who was trying to
gather information on the attitudes of young
people. The money was devised as a method to
motivate the youth to attend both sessions.

We see this data as a somewhat exploratory
way of defining appropriate targets for the
police training program. One of the most
conspicuous finding was that many of the youth
workers - given the same kinds of questions and
the same instructions - spent 30-50% longer
interviewing the youth than did the police officers.
We took a closer look at this by counting the
numer of half seconds units of speech made by
each interviewer and respondent for each question.
We then averaged across questions to get typical
speaking time/topic for each pair. It is quite
clear that the youth did a lot more talking
when interviewed by the youth-workers. Some of
this was probably due to the interrogation
style used by the police.

Although it was possible to make a
subjective judgment about their approach, we
felt it would be most useful to look at this
situation through measurable targets. We had
an observer count the number of times each
interviewer reflected, echoed, or summarized
the youth's previous response; the number of
times the interviewer responded with a positive
or a negative comment; the number of time he
expressed a personal attitude or opinion. We
also measured an interviewer's tendency to ask
questions based on the youth's previous answers.
Each of these variables was defined according
to a discrete set of behaviors whose presence
or absence was rated by the observers. By
precisely defining our measures by a set of
"behavior rules" we were able to obtain a high
percentage of interjudge agreement (93 percent

on the average).

Thus far, our data suggests that there
were differences in the "style" of various
interviewers which tended to distinguish our
police officers, as a group, from the youth
workers. The police officers did more echoing,
or summarizing, of a youth's responses, and
each tended to make at least one negative comment.
Youth workers, in contrast, made many more positive
responses to a youth, and interjected a good deal
more of their own personal attitudes and opinions
within the interview. Also, they would dwell
to a greater extent on what the youth had said,
rather than probe forward for new information.

Our most useful data pertains to the
individual performance of the various interviewers.
As expected, we found differences in the abilities
of the police officers in the interview situations.
Some officers related on a spontaneous, personal
basis with the youth, while others behaved in
a more formal, interrogation like style. We
intend to integrate these findings into training
objectives. We also have a means of conducting
a posttreatment assessment of our intervention
program, in terms of change on these particular
question and answer variables.

Having developed a strategy to define
targets, it remains for us to establish individual-
ized training programs. A number of intervention
techniques (among them role playing, practice,
video-tape feedback) can be employed in this
phase of the program.

Some training techniques are suggested
by the earlier examples, i.e., providing the
officers with systematic feedback relating to
their interview performance, by suggesting different ways to respond, prompting them with cues, etc.
The essential point is that we will relate to
measurable targets - aspects of the officer's

behavior we can count, graph, and on which we can determine change.   Our method is essentially the same, being systematic as we introduce new interventions to influence particular target behaviors.

The purpose of these illustrations have been to suggest that behavior analysis is actually a simple strategy that can make many programs more effective.   The time it takes to define a situation in measurable ways and systematically record events is very small compared to the yield.   What follows is a capsule formula of applied behavior analysis, which can be applied to any program:

1.   Define problems in practical terms in operations which can be measured in a reliable manner.   Formulate behavioral objectives or targets for these terms.

2.   Find a way to systematically record the natural frequency or base-level of these targets: either by on hand to record their occurrence, or devise a way to simulate conditions where the target behaviors are most likely to occur.

3.   Look for the environmental consequences which might make the target behavior more (or less) likley to occur, so that they can be varied in an effort to change the frequency with which these behaviors occur.

4.   Apply those conditions to your situation.   Measure the results according to changes in your target behaviors.   Graph the results.

5.   Compare the intervention to your baseline data.   If you are not satisfied with the effect, introduce another condition which you suppose will influence your target behavior.

6. And most important, keep systematically changing environmental consequences until the overall objective is obtained.

It is inconceivable that a program formulated on a systematic behavior analysis could lack an evaluation. Evaluation is the very nature of the strategy: the precise definition of goals in measurable terms, clear specification of base rates, definition and application of intervention strategies which are operationally defined, and *direct* observation of the effect of the intervention condition on the target behavior. Such an approach has revolutionized psychology, psychiatry, education and rehabilitation. We feel the time is right to revolutionize public affairs!

REFERENCES

Baer, D., Wolf, M., and Risley, T. Some current dimensions of applied behavior analysis. *Journal of Applied Behavior Analysis,* 1968, 1, 91-97.

Birnbrauer, J. S., Burchard, J.D., and Burchard, S.N. Wanted: behavior analysts. In R. H. Bradfield (ed.), *Behavior Modification, a Most Human Endeavor,* San Rafael, California: Dimension, 1969.

Hall, R.V., Panyan, M., Rabon, D., and Broden, M. Instructing beginning teachers in reinforcement procedures which improve classroom control. *Journal of Applied Behavior Analysis,* 1968, 1, 315-322.

Vorenberg, J., Quoted in *Science News,* 1966, 90, 305.

Wahler, R.G., Winkel, G.H., Peterson, R.F., and Morrison, D.C. Mothers as behavior therapists for their own children. *Behavior Research and Therapy,* 1965, 3, 113-124.

10. SOCIAL ISOLATION AND QUALITY OF LAW ENFORCEMENT

Robert E. Tournier

One of the basic tenets of Community Psychology is that it is not possible to understand an individual's behavior without considering the environmental context in which that individual exists. In his paper on social isolation and law enforcement, Robert E. Tournier describes the social position of the police officer in relation to the society he is serving. He believes that a combination of variables, including societal attitudes toward law enforcement and the nature of a police officer's social control responsibilities, have contributed to creating a position of isolation for the law enforcement officer. Tournier then presents data suggesting that this position of isolation appears to have an impact on the officer's attitude and performance.

If we are to engage in a genuine attempt at improving police-community relations, it would be useful to consider seriously the implications of social isolation which are presented in this paper. Cosmetic approaches to community relations are bound to fail. The only programs which have a chance of succeeding are those that address themselves to re-structuring the roles of police officers in relation to the communities in which they are expected to function.

171

Introduction

One issue of continual concern both to
social scientists and to those associated with
agencies of social control is that police officers
tend to be isolated from the community which
they serve.[1] On a structural level this is to
some extent an operational necessity; for while
police in a democratic society simply cannot
be permitted to become completely isolated,
effective social control necessitates a high
degree of insulation from their "clients." As
important as this is, it is not our immediate
concern; for by isolation we suggest the
existence of not only a structural but also an
interactional variable. The police, we would
suggest, can be said to be isolated when the
relationships between themselves and the
citizenry "are less frequent or of a different
nature than...thought to be desirable." [2]

Forces which create isolation originate
not only within the community, but also within
the police organization itself. While there
is no doubt that definite and significant
public rejection of interaction with police
exists, much of the isolation about which the
police complain and with which we are concerned
is the result of police-initiated behavior.
The reasons are manifold and complex, but
generally stem from the special relationship
of the police officer to morals and to law.

One of the fundamental bases of human
interaction is the reward potential associated
with it.[3] When one interacts, therefore, one
does so with an expectation of reward. For the
police officer, however, this is an intolerable
situation, because to administer the law imparti-
ally, the police officer must ideally remain
absolutely detached from potentially entangling
relationships. Indiscriminate interaction,

particularly with "outsiders," must therefore
be rejected. While this might seem to suggest
a patently utopian situation, it must be
remembered that many such actions are often
within the realm of the illegal rather than the
merely potentially compromising, and are
therefore manifestly proscribed by law.

Many police officers come to feel that
the only persons with whom they can freely
interact are other police officers, since these
represent the only individuals who will not
normally seek to compromise each other's
integrity. Rather than having to cope with the
necessity of compartmentalizing their world into
on-the-job and off-the-job sectors, many officers
combine the two and associate only with those
with whom they share this problem. They, in
effect, seek out social situations within which
they can be truly "backstage," where they can
drop their front and step out of character
without fear of censure. Here one's fellow
officers provide a safe environment, particularly
in that the establishment of a sort of reciprocity
is seen as hightly functional.

Even assuming a willingness to interact
with "outsiders," it is well to recall that, in
a sense, police officers are stigmatized by their
role and by the symbols of authority which they
bear. Their role, a role which they can only
partially relinquish, marks them as someone
dangerous, someone whose presence serves as a
reminder of omnipresent moral authority.[4]

Forces which isolate police in our society
exist not only within the realm of interaction.
In addition, police must cope with a stereotype
which characterizes them as incompetent, brutal
and corrupt. No longer is the police officer
considered a neighborhood fixture, a part of the
world within which an individual lives. He is

now, in the name of efficiency and professionalization,[5] a nameless, faceless symbol of
authority, whose infrequent contacts with the
citizenry, particularly the disadvantaged and
members of racial and ethnic minorities, often
leave a residue of resentment and distrust.
The only context within which the average citizen
encounters the police is traffic enforcement, a
task which is enormously disliked by most police
officers, as most citizens regard being cited
for a traffic violation as an unwarranted and
wholly unnecessary intrustion upon their private
interests (although traffic enforcement officers
always seem to have a repertoire of "he shook
my hand and thanked me for giving him a ticket"
stories). They are likely to react by questioning
the nature of the "proper" police function. Thus:
"Why aren't you out catching criminals?" is
continually mentioned as a reaction to receiving
a ticket.

One result of these forces is a world view
characterized by an extreme defensive cynicism:[6]
the police officer comes to think of himself as
a pariah. He comes to perceive himself and his
colleagues as members of a sort of minority group,
scorned and rejected because of erroneous stereotypes which they are powerless to change. It
should be no surprise then, that often "...the
patrolman's loyalties to his department and his
colleagues are...stronger than those to the
wider society,"[7] that police often support one
another, right or wrong, and when threatened,
fall back onto the support not of the wider
society but of the subculture of which they are
a part.

There is another result of isolation --
one which is of more importance to agencies of
law enforcement -- for it is possible to
suggest and demonstrate that perception of this
isolation by police officers leads not only to

a deterioration of attitudes consistent with good law enforcement, but also to a decline in the overall quality of law enforcement itself. We have, therefore, focused our attention upon isolation and its relationship to job satisfaction, alienation, attitude toward the law, and to a number of categories of arrest.

Research Procedures

Data for this discussion were obtained as part of a larger study of the role of reference group identification in the exercise of discretion in law enforcement. Members of the uniformed patrol force of the New Orleans Police Department, randomly selected, were used as subjects, and as such were asked to complete a questionnaire eliciting both attitudinal and behavioral data. The sample consisted of 108 subjects.

Since it was assumed that isolation would be reflected in more or less overt rejection by those with whom one comes into contact, the operationalization of this variable was approached by considering the sort of action which might be undertaken by a police officer to preclude rejection and the dissonance attendant upon it. The question was thus asked: "Do you try to hide the fact that you are a police officer from nonpolice friends and neighbors?" This, scored in a Likert fashion, was used as the primary measure of isolation.

Our choice of a measure of alienation was dictated to a great degree by convention. The concept, as it is usually employed in empirical research, has tended to be operationalized in terms of Nettler's Alienation Scale,[8] a 17-item Likert type instrument. It was in this manner that we operationalized alienation.

Job satisfaction was operationalized by

the use of a 40 item Thurstone--type instrument[9] which focuses upon belief in the law as necessary to society and to stable social living.

The categories of arrest chosen for use in the study were felonies, misdemeanors, and what was labelled "other municipal arrests." This latter category includes primarily arrests for certain types of so-called victimless crime (prostitution, "B" drinking, pornography, certain types of gambling) and for the violation of municipal licensing ordinances. The data were obtained from District Monthly Summary sheets for each officer, for a period of two months.

Findings

The various data were arranged into contigency tables from which the Q measure of association and the chi-square test of significance were derived.

TABLE I: Social Isolation/Attitude Toward The Law

Attitude Toward the Law	Social Isolation	
	Low	High
Low	53.6% (44)	73.0% (19)
High	46.4% (38)	27.0% (7)

$Q = -.402;\ x^2 = 3.05;\ p= .08$ at 1 df.

There exists a generally significant inverse relationship between social isolation and the police officer's attitude toward the law. This is most apparent for those high in isolation, where some 73 per cent of this group manifest a tendency toward a deprecation of the law as an instrument of social control.

TABLE II: Social Isolation/Job Satisfaction

Job Satis- faction	Social Isolation	
	Low	High
Low	54.9% (45)	80.8% (21)
High	45.1% (37)	19.2% (5)

$$Q = -.551; \quad x^2 = 5.58; \quad p = .02 \text{ at } 1df.$$

There exists a significant inverse
relationship between social isolation and the
police officer's satisfaction with his job.
Of those high in isolation, an overwhelming
proportion are low in satisfaction, while of
those low in isolation, roughly as many are
satisfied as are low in satisfaction.

TABLE III: Social Isolation/Alienation

Alienation	Social Isolation	
	Low	High
Low	48.7% (40)	26.9% (7)
High	51.3% (42)	73.1% (19)

$$Q = .442; \quad x^2 = 3.82; \quad p = .05 \text{ at } 1 \text{ df.}$$

There exists a significant positive
relationship between social isolation and the
police officer's sense of alienation. While
there is essentially no difference in the level
of alienation for those low in social isolation,
those high in isolation appear to be overwhelmingly alienated: almost three-quarters are high
in alienation.

TABLE IV: Social Isolation/Felony Arrests

| Felony | Social Isolation | |
Arrests	Low	High
Low	60.9% (50)	61.5% (16)
High	39.1% (32)	38.5% (10)

$Q = -.011; x^2 = .10; p = .90$ at 1 df.

There is little variance in the level of
felony arrests as a function of social isolation.
The distributions for such arrests for conditions
of both high and low social isolation are
virtually identical.

TABLE V: Social Isolation/Misdeameanor Arrests

| Misdemeanor | Social Isolation | |
Arrests	Low	High
Low	79.2% (65)	80.7% (21)
High	20.8% (17)	19.3% (5)

$Q = .05; x^2 = .10; p = .90$ at 1 df.

There is little variance in the level
of misdemeanor arrests as a function of social
isolation.   The distributions for such arrests
for conditons of both high and low social
isolation are virtually identical.

TABLE VI: Social Isolation/Municipal Arrests

| Municipal | Social Isolation | |
Arrests	Low	High
Low	41.5% (34)	73.02% (19)
High	58.5% (48)	27.0% (7)

$Q = -.586; X^2 = 7.89; p = .01$ at 1 df.

There exists a significant inverse relationship between social isolation and the level of arrests for municipal offenses. Clearly the low isolation - high arrest/ high isolation - low arrest diagonal is responsible for the largest portion of the statistical association between the variables in question.

Discussion

The modern police officer, as a result of a variety of isolating forces, is estranged from his work and from the society which he is sworn to protect and serve. As a result of isolation from and rejection by the citizenry, many police officers grow alienated and cynical. Unable to participate to full measure in the society of which they are a part, many seemingly have drawn back from it, and have created a society of their own, a society bound together by a shared occupational stigmatization. They have ceased enjoying their work, for the rewards and reinforcements which should normally attend a job well done have come to be replaced by scorn and ridicule and rejection. To realize this, is of crucial importance to police administrators, for it suggests that far from being the result, as many feel, of the financial position of the police officer, lack of job satisfaction, low morale, and a high turnover in law enforcement personnel are at least partially the result of the operation of structural variables endemic to the position of the police officer in our society.

Another manifestation of this is an unhappiness with and an apparent rejection of the law as an instrument of social control. Far from seeing the law as an articulation of social norms, many police officers, isolated from external input, have adopted a wholly

practical, wholly pragmatic view of the law as
a weapon to be wielded in the name of the judicial
system. This is not to suggest that police
officers reject the law or engage in activities
which transcend legality; it is to suggest that
many law enforcement officers have adopted,
as the result of their relative isolation, a
perspective on the law which may be inappro-
priately narrow.

This is most manifest when we leave the
realm of attitude and enter the realm of behavior,
for one result of the perception of isolation
by police officers appears to be in the
emergence of selectivity in the enforcement
of law. In situations where criminality is
unequivocal, there is absolutely no variation
in enforcement as a function of isolation.
This, of course, is as it should be. In areas
of borderline criminality, however, areas
designated as illegal as an articulation of
societal ideals, there emerges a significant
pattern of underenforcement by those high in
isolation.

The cause of this, we feel, lies in an
inappropriate exercise of discretion by isolated
police officers who, reacting to a sense of
estrangement from society, have come to restrict
their attention to that which is patently
criminal, placing that which is perceived as
only marginally criminal in a lower priority
position. This is not necessarily bad law
enforcement per se, for no one would deny the
necessity of having to allocate scarce resources
to the most important enforcement areas. It
is open to criticism, however, on the grounds
that these allocation decisions seem to be
made for the wrong reasons by the wrong
individuals.

The issue is ultimately one of

responsiveness; responsiveness not only by the police to citizen demands, but also responsiveness by citizens to the need of integrating police into the fabric of the community. Currently a large proportion of the public relations/ human relations efforts of police departments are given over to breaking down the barriers which separate the police from racial and ethnic minorities. This is as it should be, but in an effort to mend one sort of bridge others have been allowed to fall into disrepair.

To make relevant recommendations is always a difficult task, as general recommendations rarely bear any relationship to the specific problems faced in particular settings. There are, however, a number of general points which can be made. In an effort to depoliticize the police, we have, in the eyes of many, dehumanized them. In an effort to set the police above their constituency, we have set them apart.

Efforts must be made to reintegrate the police: by taking the police officer out of the car, not in the name of better law enforcement, but in an attempt to have him perceived as more than a faceless symbol of impersonal authority; by assigning traffic enforcement responsibilities to a separately constituted, separately uniformed organization; and most importantly, by putting the police back into the community, not as law officers, but as citizens committed to the maintenance of order.

FOOTNOTES

1. John P. Clark, "Isolation of the Police: A
    Comparison of the British and American
    Situation," *Journal of Criminal Law,
    Criminology and Police Science,*LVI
    (September 1965, 307 FF. See also:
    William Turner, *The Police Establishment*
    (New York: Putnam and Sons, 1968), p.15;
    Michael Banton, *The Policeman in the
    Community* (New York: Basic Books, Inc.,
    1964), pp. 166 ff.; Jerome H. Skolnick,
    *Justice Without Trial: Law Enforcement in
    Democratic Society* (New York: John Wiley
    and Sons, 1967), pp. 49-61.

2. Clark, *op. cit.,* p. 307.

3. George C. Homans, *Social Behavior: Its
    Elementary Forms* (New York: Harcourt, Brace
    and World, Inc.,1961), pp. 35ff. He defines
    interaction almost exclusively in terms of
    reciprocity of reward. Thus: "When an
    activity...emitted by one man is rewarded..
    by an activity emitted by another..we say
    that the two have interacted."

4. Clark suggests an alternative explanation for
    this, that police officers tend to be set
    apart because they represent "visible
    reminders of the seamy and recalcitrant
    portions of human behavior." (Clark,
    op. cit., p. 308.) While this is undoubted-
    ly true to some extent, it seems an in-
    adequate explanation for the persistence
    with which social contacts with police
    are rejected.

5. While professionalization is often proposed
    as a solution to many of the problems
    associated with law enforcement, there is
    at least a possiblity that it may tend to
    further aggravate an already sensitive

situation by creating an image of
"unapproachability." (Clark, *op. cit.*,
p. 308.

6. The most important contribution to the study
of this area of cynicism and its relationship to the world view of the police officer
is, of course, Arthur Niederhoffer, *Behind
the Shield: The Police in Urban Society*
(Garden City, N.Y.: Doubleday and Co.,Inc.,
1967), pp. 187-242.

7. Banton, *op. cit.* p. 170.

8. Gwynn Nettler, "A Measure of Alienation,"
American Sociological Review, XXII (December
1957), 670-677. The scale itself is to be
found on p. 675.

9. Marvin E. Shaw and Jack M. Wright, *Scales for
the Measurement of Attitudes* (New York:
McGraw-Hill Book Co.,1967), pp. 249-251.

SECTION V:

SUMMARY AND CONCLUSIONS

11. SUMMATION OF CRITICAL ISSUES FOR SOCIAL SCIENTISTS WORKING WITH POLICE AGENCIES

Charles W. Dean

Charles Dean is able to view the relationship between police and social scientists from a unique position. His perspective has been enriched by his dual experiences as the director of a correctional facility for delinquent boys, and as a sociologist in a university setting. Having served in both roles, he is better able to avoid over identifying with either profession.

At the Symposium on Working With Police Agencies, Dean served as an observer - summarizer. He attended all of the sessions in an effort to synthesize the major themes, issues and problems which appeared to exist in the relationships between police and social scientists. At the conclusion of the symposium he present his over-all impressions to the entire group of participants. Both police and social scientists seemed to agree with most of his observations.

The following paper is an adaptation of Charles Dean's concluding presentation. It has been modified in order to be applicable to a broader range of agencies and relationships than those represented at the symposium.

The present complex role of the policeman
has developed over the years by adding functions
needed at certain times and places, with little
thought of the end product. New laws are passed
with little concern for their enforceability
or their effect on the law enforcement agency.
In many instances, law enforcement personnel are
assigned new duties with little guidance about
how to allocate time if some portion of the
officers job must be left undone.

Defining the role of the policeman reminds
one of the art of grafting of fruit trees.
Branches of various fruit can be grafted onto
the trunk of still another kind of fruit. The
end product of the grafted branches is unlike
the end product of either part before the graft.
After over two centuries of grafting new parts
onto the role of the policeman, the end product
is, indeed, a complicated, often inconsistent,
sometimes almost impossible role with high and
increasing expectations.

This complicated role is most suitable
for study by any one of several academic disciplines.
A lengthy and intense discussion between policemen
and social science practitioners at the synposium
on Working with Police Agencies resulted in a
rather substantial list of areas that were of
mutual interest. These are outlined briefly
below.

1) On the one hand police organizations
typically have a quasi - military organizational
structure. On the other hand, increasingly,
police are called upon to perform work that
requires a mental health perspective. Specific
examples of this are the juvenile squads, as
well as the family counseling which has been
formalized as an official part of some policemen's duties. The problem of a mental health
task in a military organizational structure is

also characteristic of correctional institutions.
Neither police nor correctional agencies have
addressed themselves to the consequences of the
inherent conflicts that arise from this situation.
A mental health worker has a professional
relationship to a client which on certain levels
requires privileged communication. A policeman
is required to counsel at times, but if his
counseling should lead in the right direction,
it may result in a report which will be used as
evidence in a court hearing. This dual role
could result in the person viewing the policeman
as dishonest and treacherous. The placing of
indigenous forces in slum neighborhoods reflects
problems faced by a policeman if they attempt
to act on every instance of law violation they
encounter. The organization requires an arrest
for local offense, but the community would not
understand referring neighbors to outsiders.
Many policemen are extremely sensitive and
effective interviewers and develop close relations
with the people they serve. It would be
advantageous to understand whether the policemen,
the police supervisor, or the client sees these
roles as contradictory. If the policeman chooses
to intervene in a situation or in another person's
life in other than the role of a law enforcement
agent, what impact does this have on his role
as a policeman and as an employee of an agency
with a military structure?

2) There has been much discussion of the
unrelatedness of pre-service training to the
actual day to day work of a policeman. It has
frequently been said that the real training occurs
when the new policeman gets in the car with an
experienced officer. While there has been
considerable effort to make training more
relevant, only recently has there been literature
available on the way a policeman actually spends
his time. Readjusting training to the actual
task the policeman performs still lags behind
and needs increased attention.

3) In any organization, there usually
is considerable variation in the perceptions of
an individual's role, depending on the level in
the organizational hierachy that the perceiver
occupies. Discussions among police representatives
suggest that the police patrolman's perceptions of
his role may be unlike the perceptions his
supervisors have of that same role. The reverse
of this might also be true. This might account
for some of the negative attitudes patrolmen
sometimes have toward training, since the
training would be planned and conducted by a
person who does not perceive of the patrolman's
role the way he sees it. Even though
practically all superiors have at one time been
patrolmen, this does not necessarily insure
that, once promoted, the supervisor retains
an accuracte perception of the role he previously held. Certain parts of that role become more
important to him in his supervisory position
and these might well receive emphasis to the
neglect of what the patrolman himself thinks
is more important.

4) From the wide range of expectations
faced by a police agency or an individual, certain
of these expectations are ranked above others,
either implicitly or explicitly. Any role or
organization has a paramount value system and
this is true of police agencies as well.
Perceptions of this value system vary by position
in the organization or by rank in a police
agency. The emphasized values may shift with
time and circumstances in a rather unpredictable
fashion, so that what is considered most
important today may not be considered most
important a month later. For example, after an
incident where a policeman has been accused
of using excessive force to make an arrest, it
may be more important to maintain good community
relations than to follow the letter of the law;
whereas after a series of much publicized and

serious crimes, the reverse may be true.   Among
the various expectations such as community
relations, enforcement of law, loyalty to
superiors, maintaining order in an area,
completing paperwork, personal appearance,etc.,
which is most consistently expected of a
policeman? Is he judged by the number of
arrests, by the number of community complaints,
by the problems he presents to superior himself,
by his ability to solve difficult cases, etc.?

5) There is general agreement that
rewards are very scarce in police agencies.
Under these circumstances small benefits and
rewards tend to become valued more highly than
they would under other circumstances. What do
police officers at various levels see as the
rewards for doing their job well? Is it the
extracurricular activities, the fringe benefits,
the respect they get from certain parts of the
community, the feeling that they have for
rendering community service, the relationships
they have with co-workers? The work of a policeman is dangerous, the hours are irregular and
the status is low. If there were a greater
understanding of the policeman's perception of
the benefits of his job, it would be well to
utilize these to increase overall job
satisfaction.

6) Every organization has difficulty
with the filtering of information as it goes up
through the chain of command. One of the most
difficult tasks of a top administrator is
finding out what happens on line levels. In
large police forces, this is an extremely
difficult task. The New York City Police
Department presently is undergoing a massive
decentralization in an effort to gain more
control of the functioning of partrolmen.
What kind of information is it that is filtered
out and what kind of information is allowed

to go up through the chain of command? What
is the relevance of this official information
to the overall day-to-day functioning of a
policeman?

7) There has been a general tendency in
all fields toward specialization of roles.
This is true of police agencies as well. As
different policmen are assigned to specific
tasks such as family relations, community
relations, planning, or juvenile services, what
effect does this have on the overall functioning
of the police department? These roles will
become arranged inevitably in some kind of a
status hierarchy and this hierarchy will in
turn affect the overall functioning of the
agency,as well as the morale of the people in
it. If the brunt of the burden for law
enforcement falls on the patrolman while others
are performing specialized tasks which are not
so directly related to law enforcement, are
the rewards arranged accordingly?

8) The rate of promotion among
policemen is very low. Recently in Connecticut
the State Police gave a test for promotion to
sergeant. Two hundred-twenty-five passed the
test for which there were 17 vacancies. These
figures may be slightly exaggerated but the
chances for promotion to the upper levels of
a police agency are slim as indicated by the
number of line staff as compared with the
number of administrative staff. There have
been numerous studies in other types of
organizations relative to the consequences of
low promotion potential. Automobile workers
initially expect promotion or to leave the
factory for a small business or other jobs.
After a period of time they reconcile themselves
to their position, seeking gratification in areas
other than their work, and view their work as
a less important part of their life. No

similar studies have been performed on the
effects of a low promotion potential among
policemen. Perhaps the moonlighting of many
policemen may be an adjustment to this.

9) There is indication of increasing
concern for the family situaion of the
policeman. Some claim that the divorce rate
is very high among policemen, whereas others
indicate that the rate is no higher than the
other groups. There has been a considerable
amount of research on the adjustment of wives
of clergymen and other occupational groups.
The policeman's problems with his family
relationships has been recognized by some
agencies as they have offered free psychological
counseling with the families of their officers,
and some agencies have held seminars for wives.
The policeman works frequently in rotating
shifts and his work gives him high public
exposure in addition to the constant awareness
of danger. Research is needed to ascertain the
extent of marital difficulties among policemen
and whether family problems are associated with
the role of the police officer.

10) Community relations teams are
becoming a more common part of a police department. Some policemen indicated that they use
the community relations team as a dumping
ground for officers who are not good in their
work. One Captain admitted that when he was
told to give up one man for the community
relations team, he sent the worst man he had.
It would be expected that at some point there
will be a general evaluation of the effectiveness
of community relations units. If most police
agencies send their less competent people,
then it would not be reasonable to expect
great success.

11) What is the relationship of the

police to other community agencies as reflected
in the preservice orientation, inservice
training and the day-to-day operation of the
police. Police frquently deal with people who
eventually are referred to mental health
agencies, juvenile court, welfare agencies,
etc. What preparation does the police have for
this and of what assistance is the administration
in acquainting them with the resources available
to them if they decide to refer rather than
perform a traditional law-enforcement role?

12) There is some indication that some
police think they do not need training. There
is little indication as to how strongly police
officers feel about this, or how many of them
feel training is not something required for the
kind of work they do. The perception of the
line police officer toward training, in terms
of type of training needed and whether training
is needed at all, has been neglected and is
requisite to effective planning for training.

13) The policeman has one of the few
jobs that requires constant confrontation with
people with whom he does not maintain contact
over a long period of time. A foreman or
supervisor may have to confront staff occasionally,
but generally relationships are long-lived and
relatively harmonious. The policeman confronts
strangers as a matter of his daily routine.
If these confrontations are not handled
adequately, many of them could develop into
serious incidents. There is little information
as to the overall effect of the constant
confrontation a policeman experiences in the
course of his day's work. If a policeman
enjoys confrontation, this effect might be
altogether different than it would be for a
policeman who is not comfortable during a
confrontation situation. There is little
evidence to provide guidelines as to the

consequences of constant confrontation and ways
of dealing with problems that might result
from this in other areas of the officer's life.

14) Generally, police agencies like all
other organizations, tend to resist change.
This is not due to selecting a particularly
obstinate type of person, but rather to social
and cultural circumstances in which the police
agency finds itself. These conditions include
the relative status of police agencies in the
criminal justice heirarchy, the social status
ascribed to the role of policemen, contradictory
pressures resulting in the realm of public
expectations of policemen and police agencies,
etc. There has been little attention to the
structured social and cultural sources of
resistance to change in police agencies.

15) There has been a considerable emphasis
on hiring professionals as policemen. One well -
published project was considered successful
because it was able to recruit and made it
possible for an agency to recruit a large number
of college graduates as policemen. Other areas
of the criminal justice system are finding that
the younger college graduate has at least as
much difficulty in his work as does the noncollege
graduate of the same age. There has been little
study on the relationship between educational
attainment and the conduct of the police officer.
The question of how best to professionalize a
police force remains unanswered.

16) There has been little study on the
erosive effects of the constant exposure to
human problems and weaknesses that the policeman
encounters day after day. Policemen are known
to be aware of the tremendous amount of
hypocrisy in the system, and to face daily the
task of knowing who to arrest and not to arrest
because of their influence or lack of influence.

In addition, the people with whom the policeman is most likely to deal are the least reputable socially and when he encounters those who are more reputable there is little mutual respect.

17) There are hundreds of calls to a police station in the course of an average week. Meeting the needs which precipitate these calls requires a diversity of personnel. There has been little investigation regarding methods of classifying these calls as to the incident involved, the time of day, the day of the week, etc. Also there is little information about who called and whether or not there is follow-up and whether the caller feels appropriate action has been taken.

18) There has been considerable experimen-tation with police wearing different types of uniforms. Yet there has been little systematic study of the consequences of wearing a uniform or not wearing a uniform.

19) The high visibility of the policeman makes him highly vulnerable to criticism from the public. Probably no other occupational category is said to have such indirect supervision from their superiors, but such intensive supervision by the community. This relates closely to the feedback problems of the adminis-trator and needs thorough study, description and analysis.

20) There has been nationwide publicity on the involvement of policemen in family fights. One study showed that police injuries were more likely to occur when the police were involved in this kind of situation, than in other situations which might be presumed to be more serious. Without question, there are numerous other patterns in which policeman are most likely to be injured, when the image of the police agency

is most likely to be at stake, or when the
policeman feels unprepared to deal with the
situation. There have been studies on when
the police use violence and these have turned
out to be rather unflattering to the police
agency. Aside from those studies focusing on
when police use violence and when physical
injury is most likely to occur, there are
numerous other recurring problems that need
to be identified, classified and investigated.

21) There is a large body of literature
on the role of a consultant in the mental health
field. There have been large grants to study
the role and effectiveness of consultants.
There is virtually no such literature in the
criminal justice field. There has been
considerable discussion, some of it controversial,
as to the role of a consultant in a police agency.
Some maintain that the consultant should maintain
objectivity and avoid any kind of administrative
or personal involvement, while others maintain
that effective consultation requires involvement.

The above paragraphs represent topics
which appear to be of mutual interest to both
social and behavioral scientists, as well as
police officers. They are also areas which
pose major problems that have not been adequately
researched. Without doubt, there are many
other areas which could be added to this list
and each of the above represents only rough
hypotheses. Further refinement of the
statements is needed. The greatest need is
for relevant disciplines to focus attention on
the problems that police agencies encounter
daily. Many of the problems are not unique to
police agencies and have as much theoretical
potential as research in any other kind of
organization. Police departments are sometimes
less receptive to outside researchers than are
other organizations and social scientists will

not find a wealth of prior research to guide
their study, but there is urgent need to
answer the questions. Before answers to
vital questions are likely to be forthcoming,
both police administrators and social science
researchers will have to bite the bullet of
objective, theoretically based relevant
research in the area of law enforcement.

12. FINAL CONSIDERATIONS

Robert P. Sprafkin and Robert Cohen

The preceding chapters have dealt with many aspects of the working relationship between social science practitioners and police. Some authors have drawn attention to the personal and philosophical issues that ought to be considered by both police officials and social scientists; other authors have described the types of service which practitioners might render to police agencies; and others have been concerned with the strategies and methods that may be utilized to reduce obstacles, and facilitate the implementation of cooperative efforts.

While the material presented covers a wide range of ideas and programs related to working with police, there are several basic concepts and themes that appear throughout the book. In most instances, these are presented as ideas or principles to be considered, rather than absolute dictums to be followed. For this reason, these fundamental issues are summarized below in the form of questions that might be asked by social scientists and police officials who are contemplating the development of a collaborative effort.

1. *Basic Considerations for Both Social*

Scientists and Police

- What do you expect to gain from this relationship?
- What are the potential risks and liabilities of this relationship?
- What do you expect to contribute?
- What do you expect of your counterpart in the relationship, police or social science practitioner?
- Have you communicated your expectations clearly and explicitly to those you will be working with at the beginning of the project?
- Do you have personal values which may impede or facilitate the development of a collaborative relationship? What are they and how might you deal with these values to enhance your effectiveness?
- Do you have preconceptions about your counterpart in the relationship? What are they?
- What skills do you bring to this relationship? What skills do you feel you need to upgrade?
- Have you considered the potential impact of your work on people or forces other than those primarily involved? Have you attempted to orient and enlist the support of those people who are capable of affecting your efforts?
- Who are you going to be responsive to? Who are you accountable to?
- Are you committed to this collaborative effort?
- Have you finalized mutually acceptable contractual arrangements?
- How are you going to assess the effectiveness of your efforts?
- Have you made adequate provisions for follow-up?

2. *Basic Considerations for Social Science Practitioners*

   - Have you given the law enforcement officials you intend to work with a realistic picture of the scope and limitations of your skills and services?
   - Have you developed an entry process plan that will enable you to minimize resistance and maximize your chances for gaining acceptance and credibility?
   -Do you have an adequate understanding of the social systems in which you will be involved?
   - In developing your services and programs have you taken into account all aspects of the law enforcement system and local community that are related to the area of police work you will be involved in? Are these people and groups committed to this program?
   - Have you assessed whether your services may have a long term impact, or whether they will merely have a superficial or temporary effect on the police agency? Is your work primarily academic or practical?

3. *Basic Considerations for the Police Officer or Official*

   - Do you understand the potential benefits and limitations of social science assistance?
   - Do you have an accurate picture of the needs of your agency and how the proposed social science services relate to those needs?
   - Have you cleared this collaborative effort with all appropriate people?
   - If you are an administrator, do the people you are responsible for understand and accept the project? If you are a direct

service officer, do you feel your
superiors are committed to this project?
- Do you feel that the project has been
designed so that you will have an
effective voice in determining what will
happen?
- How will you know when this project is
successful or unsuccessful? When should
it be terminated?

It seems ironic that the present text both
begins and ends with questions. In the introduction
we addressed ourselves to broad questions concerning the possibility of even holding a working
dialogue between police and social scientists.
In these concluding remarks we are confronted
with more specific, sophisticated questions.
In reading through these latter questions, one
can almost envision them as a checklist to be
responded to by police and social scientists who
are contemplating a collaborative effort. This
refinement of the questions seems to capture the
essence of the process discussed in previous
chapters. It means, perhaps, that we are not
yet equipped to offer definitive answers. If,
however, we have reached that stage where we are
asking the right questions of ourselves and our
counterparts, it is fair to say we've come a
long way.